Advance Praise for *A P*

"Although much has been written about the Lost Boys of Sudan who resettled in large groups in the United States beginning in 2000, very little, if anything, has been written about the countless Sudanese who fled alone to neighboring countries such as Egypt in an effort to escape the civil war between north and south Sudan ... until now.

"For the first time, Judy Pex breaks the silence, unfolding the perilous journey of Sudanese refugees that fled to Egypt only to find continued hardships and persecution, which ultimately led them to make the dangerous choice of illegally crossing the Egyptian border in search of a better life in Israel. For many, it was a choice that came at tremendous cost: imprisonment, separation from their children and spouses, hunger, brutal beatings and death. It's a story of resilience, determination and the choice for freedom—at all cost."

Joan Hecht, award-winning author of *The Journey of the Lost Boys*

"The breadth and depth of the book is quite breathtaking. The style of letting refugees such as Gabriel, Yien, Rose and the two Munas relate their own stories, makes for compelling reading, relaying as they do the terrible sufferings, hardships, rejections, and fortitude of thousands of Sudanese in recent years. I first met the author and her husband, John, when I worked in Israel. Through their ministry in Eilat, Israel, the Pexes have shown a great heart of love for all who come their way, irrespective of color, creed or culture.... This book deserves a wide audience."

David Price, retired former rector of Christ Church in Jerusalem

"This spellbinding book which gives the reader a heart-wrenching look into the lives of five special human beings who have suffered incredible persecution puts a human face on the statistics we hear concerning Sudan."

Fran Boyle, Director CLIM (Connecting Lives International Mission) USA

"I am from Bintiu in south Sudan. We love the book that Judy Pex wrote. I hope those who read it will understand us Sudanese better. We love the family of Judy and John. They help us with everything."

Simon Koang, Sudanese Refugee

"Judy Pex writes with a deep understanding not only of Israel and her refugees but of human nature and God's heart for all His children. Pex will move you with her words, her details, and the experiences of those with whom she has worked. She and her husband are living examples of God's arms that are open to everyone."

Eric Wilson, *NY Times* bestselling novelist

"Sudan's civil war claimed the lives of millions and displaced far more as the mostly Muslim Arab north warred with the mostly Christian and animist south. *A People Tall & Smooth* shares the stories of Sudanese refugees who fled their nation's carnage in search of a better life and country. Their journey reminds us of the words in Hebrews 11:16, 'But now they desire a better, that is, a heavenly country...' Their stories will challenge the church to be salt and light to those seeking such a land."

Corey Odden, CEO of The Voice of the Martyrs-Canada

"Judy's ability to tell the moving and important story of the Sudanese refugees is both unusual and enjoyable. This book, which includes five personal stories, should be heard and echoed around the world. It comes at exactly the right time."

Ofir Malki, representative for ASSAF, Aid Organization for Refugees and Asylum Seekers in Israel

"An excellent book on the decades of horrific suffering inflicted upon the Sudanese people and the opportunity taken by one couple to be the hands and feet of Christ to the least and the lost at the time of thier desperate need. I find *A People Tall & Smooth* to be accurate, educational and challenging."

William N. Deans, MUSTARD SEED INTERNATIONAL

A People Tall and Smooth

Stories of Escape from Sudan to Israel

A People Tall and Smooth

Stories of Escape from Sudan to Israel

Judith Galblum Pex

CLADACH
Publishing

Published by
Cladach Publishing
PO Box 336144 Greeley, CO 80633
WWW.CLADACH.COM

Library of Congress Cataloging-in-Publication Data

Pex, Judith Galblum.
  A people tall and smooth : stories of escape from Sudan to Israel / Judith Galblum Pex.
     p. cm.
  ISBN 978-0-9818929-3-1 (pbk.)
  1. Refugees--Israel. 2. Refugees--Sudan. 3. Sudanese--Israel. 4. Sudan--History--Civil War, 1983-2005--Refugees. 5. Sudan--History--Darfur Conflict, 2003---Refugees. 6. Sudan--Emigration and immigration. 7. Israel--Emigration and immigration. I. Title.

  HV640.4.I75P49 2011
  305.9'0691409225694--dc22
  [B]
                              2011004820

ISBN-10: 0981892930
ISBN-13: 9780981892931

Printed in the United States of America

Foreword

Like most people I had heard and read about the tragedy in Darfur and the ongoing hostilities in South Sudan that have taken at least two million lives. But I had little comprehension of the terrible living conditions of the thousands of refugees from such horrors until I met them face to face in Egypt. In large numbers they have moved into some of the most pitiable slums in Cairo and somehow or other they eke out an existence there. However, in their crowded, unhygienic (I caught Typhoid) and dangerous environment we found viable, vital little churches, believers who despite their poverty dressed in their "Sunday best" to worship. And we saw Christian love on show.

Incredibly, out of their poverty these believers were reaching out to their Darfurian neighbors whose plight was worse than theirs. And remember the Sudanese from the south are "Christians" and the Darfurians are "Muslims."

Most of the people we met were glad to be in Egypt but were eager to move on, hopefully to a place where they could rebuild their lives. But permission to move was hard to come by; so I was not surprised when I heard from my friend Judy Pex in Israel that large numbers of Sudanese were making the exhausting and hazardous journey across the Sinai to Israel. "Hope," as they say, "springs eternal in the human breast"; and no doubt refugees keep on hoping longer than most.

In the case of those who reached Israel and found "The Shelter" in Eilat, many of their hopes were realized. Judy tells their story. It will gladden—and tear—your heart.

Stuart Briscoe
pastor, author, broadcaster

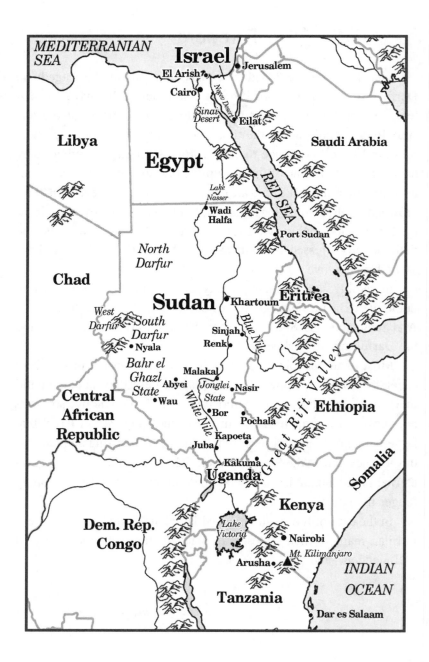

Contents

INTRODUCTION

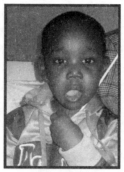

A Sudanese refugee child in Eilat, Israel

Who are They and Why Have They Come?

People from over one hundred nations intermingle in Israel. Besides Jews from Kazakhstan and Kansas, Burma and Belgrade, Calcutta, Congo and places in between, over a million tourists every year add to the mosaic. Include in the mixture two hundred thousand legal and illegal workers from countries such as China, Thailand, Philippines, Nepal and Ghana, and it's clear that the average Israeli is used to seeing faces of all colors and shapes.

In 2007, however, a new group appeared on the scene whose appearance and status was unlike any other till this time. We began to notice men, women, children and babies on the streets in our town of Eilat who were exceptionally black and strikingly tall.

"Where do they come from and who are they?" My husband John and I asked ourselves. "What language do they speak?" Having managed The Shelter Hostel in Eilat on the Red Sea since 1984, we are used to interacting with diverse people groups and were eager to meet these new arrivals.

Our questions were answered when a tall, dark man walked through our front gate one morning. "I'm Gabriel, a refugee from Sudan," he introduced himself in perfect English. We then had even more questions. How did these Sudanese get to our city of Eilat in the south of Israel? What made them want to come to Israel of all places? Were they refugees from the genocide in Darfur that we'd been reading about lately?

The next time he visited, Gabriel brought several countrymen and the connections multiplied quickly. As the Sudanese refugees became an integral part of our lives, their story gradually unfolded for us and Gabriel in time became a dear friend.

"Why did you come to Israel?" we asked Isaac, one of Gabriel's friends. Sudan, we knew, was one of the most extreme Muslim countries.

"In south Sudan we are mostly Christians," he explained. "The fanatical Muslims who hate Israel are likewise killing our people. We escaped from Egypt as the children of Israel fled from Pharaoh and his army. There's a chapter in the Bible about the Sudanese coming to Mt. Zion."

Sudanese on Mt. Zion? Although I have been reading the Bible since I came to Israel in 1973, I couldn't recall that passage.

Isaac opened a Bible to Isaiah Chapter 18 and we read:

> Woe to the land of whirring wings along the rivers of Cush, which sends envoys by sea in papyrus boats over the water. Go swift messengers to a people tall and smooth-skinned, to a people feared far and wide, an aggressive nation of strange speech whose land is divided by rivers ... At that time gifts will be brought to the Lord Almighty ... to Mount Zion.

Cush was the ancient name for Sudan. Our new friends were obviously tall as well as smooth-skinned, having little body hair. In the short time we were acquainted with them we noticed their hot tempers, which matched the description of "an aggressive nation."

"Sudan is the 'land divided by rivers' because the White and the Blue Niles meet in Khartoum, the capital," said Isaac.

Whatever the original meaning, many Sudanese took this passage as a personal encouragement in their complicated struggle as refugees in Israel. Still, life with uncertainties in Israel was better for them than what they had endured in Africa.

Due to the war in south Sudan which had been going on intermittently since 1983, thousands of Sudanese fled to Egypt, but life was difficult for them even there as Egyptians are naturally prejudiced against dark-skinned people. As refugees, they lived in the worst neighborhoods in Cairo and worked in the most menial jobs in a country where much of the native population lives in poverty and unemployment. They often weren't paid and had no recourse to collect their wages. Workers were frequently abused by bosses. If someone was sick, proper medical treatment often wasn't available.

Somehow the Sudanese hung on, partly through the hope that the United Nations would resettle them in Australia, Canada or the United States. A few had succeeded, but the process was extremely slow.

Subsequently, for many refugees, their already difficult life became unbearable. Soon the first of the current wave of refugees began making their way to Israel. They must have been desperate to take such a risk. How did they decide to cross the border illegally into an enemy state—a country of which the only news they heard in both Sudan and Egypt was negative to the extreme?

In the beginning the flow was little more than a trickle, but by June 14, 2007, Haaretz newspaper reported that up to fifty refugees each day were crossing from the Sinai into Israel, and that in the span of a month and a half, seven hundred Africans had arrived in Israel, a third being from Sudan.

When the surge began, Israel was faced with a dilemma. Sudan is an enemy state having no diplomatic relations with Israel. In the past, Sudan harbored terrorist groups including Al Qaeda and Osama Bin Laden. Enforcing the sharia law, Sudan is even today one of the most extreme Islamic states. In Israel, therefore, Sudanese citizens were considered a security threat and the government felt justified in sending the men to jail.

Yet Israel began to realize they couldn't keep stuffing prisons full of refugees. Israeli human rights organizations protested that this went against the Geneva Convention. In 1949 the young state of Israel had lobbied to have a clause added to this Convention requiring countries to differentiate between refugees from enemy countries and enemy citizens, citing the example of Jewish refugees seeking safety in England from Nazi Germany.

The Sudanese refugees found advocates in Holocaust spokesmen such as Eli Wiesel, a Holocaust survivor and Nobel laureate who protested that Israel had a moral obligation to help people fleeing from genocide, as the Darfur situation was defined.

As a result of the pressure from non-governmental agencies (NGOs) but without a clear plan or vision, the Israeli government began releasing from jail some of the refugees, to kibbutzim and moshavim where they were allowed to work. They reasoned that the refugees would be under a type of house-arrest but have the ability to reside outside of prison and to earn money.

A friend of mine was working with the Sudanese at the time. "They're happy to be out of jail, but they still don't feel free because they aren't allowed to travel outside the kibbutz," she told me. "And it's hard for them to live as a single family on the kibbutz since they're used to living in a community."

Hearing that the refugees were allowed to work in the kibbutzim, the hotel managers in Eilat, a city dependent on tourism, had a bright idea. Desperately short of workers but unable to find enough Israelis willing to work in the lowest paying jobs as dishwashers or cleaners, they reasoned that the Sudanese could fill those positions. Eilat is separated from the rest of Israel by the Negev Desert, so the Sudanese could also be considered to be under house-arrest while working in Eilat.

The government agreed and within a few weeks, in May and June of 2007, hundreds of Sudanese began arriving in Eilat and working in hotels. Gabriel was one of the first.

It appeared to be the perfect plan. The refugees received housing, meals, and even daycare for their children; and the hotels found cheap labor.

"Where else in the world do refugees have it so good?" I asked John. "In Afghanistan, Chad, Pakistan, the Congo and other places, the refugees live in deplorable conditions in tent camps or slums, while in Eilat they have jobs and apartments."

In this connected world of cell phones and email, friends and family of the refugees soon heard about the excellent conditions waiting for those who arrived in Israel. More and more refugees arrived, as well as nationals from other African countries such as Ivory Coast, Eritrea and Nigeria, who were seeking a better life for themselves and a chance to earn a higher salary than at home.

In time we realized that the hotels weren't charitable organizations with altruistic goals. In some cases the money being deducted for the refugee's expenses was more than they were making and the poor people were in debt to the hotel.

The refugees themselves and those of us who were helping them realized that Israel could in no way accommodate all the poor Africans who wanted to come here—potentially millions. But what was the solution?

We believed it was our duty to help those already in Israel and to treat each one as a human being created in God's image. We would help however we could. And we would try to understand their situation—what they came from, how they got here, and how we can help them transition into a new culture.

The heart-wrenching sagas of their dangerous, roundabout journeys from south Sudan and Darfur to Israel touched us deeply. Our lives have become so intertwined with theirs, that at the end of the day John and I often look at each other and ask, "What did we do before we met the Sudanese?"

1. GABRIEL

Gabriel in Jerusalem 2007

Into the Promised Land

*O*n a comfortable day in May Gabriel began calmly telling his story. With skin darker than almost anyone I'd ever seen, he folded his long, thin frame into an armchair in our living room. He paused and looked around the room with doleful, steady eyes. Around him, twenty five young people sat in chairs and on the floor in eager silence, straining to hear Gabriel's smooth, calm voice.

*I*f I told you everything that's happened in my life it would be too sad, so I'll make my story short. I'm about thirty years old, and I've experienced war in my home country since I was six. I haven't felt any happiness in my life.

*G*abriel was our guest at a planning session for the 2007 "Fun Day" we were organizing for Sudanese refugee children. We asked him to share his story, hoping he could help us understand the background of these children.

*T*o understand our problems, you have to know that throughout
its history, Sudan has been divided between the north with its
Arab, Muslim heritage, and the south where we are Christians (as
I am) or animists.

During Sudan's Civil War that began in 1983, government
troops from the north attacked and bombed my village in the south.
My family was separated—we all ran in different directions. Most
were killed. At that point, I was still with my mother but when
I was eleven years old I separated from her and fled with other
young boys to Ethiopia. Eventually I began wandering from place
to place in East Africa. But wherever I went, I was an outsider, a
refugee with no documents.

*A*s I listened I thought how I like to travel and have been
to many countries. But I couldn't imagine traveling without a passport. Of course I'd often read about refugees in the newspaper and
seen pictures on television of displaced people from Afghanistan,
Bosnia, Iraq and other nations. There are millions of refugees all
over the world. But I'd never realized that the simple detail of not
having a passport was enough to cause Gabriel to be thrown into
jail in nearly every country he entered.

Gabriel continued:

*I*n 2004, after wandering about for so many years looking for
a peaceful place to live and the possibility to study but with no
success, I decided to move to Egypt. Unfortunately, I discovered
that in Egypt the situation was no better than in Sudan. Gangs of
thugs attacked us Sudanese on the streets for no reason. The people
of Egypt and north Sudan all act the same toward us southerners
and hate us because of our black skin.

I was employed in Cairo as an interpreter of the Dinka
language, my mother tongue, into English for the United Nations
and the International Red Cross. But the Sudanese government

officials weren't happy with my work on behalf of the refugees from south Sudan. My life was in danger and I couldn't move about freely on the streets.

I'd heard about Sudanese crossing the border into Israel. I knew about Israel. By this time I had acquired a passport, and in it was written, 'Good for all countries of the world except for Israel.' I was aware of the dangers but I had nothing to lose and saw no other path open to me. I knew I couldn't return to Sudan.

I decided that even if Israel were an enemy state to Sudan, I would go there and tell them, 'Sudan and Israel are enemies. But the Sudanese government that's against Israel is against me too. I'm running away from that government, but they've followed me to Cairo. So please, I'm fleeing for my life. Please forget about Sudan being an enemy state and help me.'

I saved some money and traveled with a friend to El Arish in the northern Sinai. We found Bedouin guides and paid them to help us get to the border. Our first problem was Egypt's many secret police and roadblocks. Just being a Sudanese on the way to the Sinai arouses suspicion. If you're caught, they kill you or throw you into jail; or if you're really unlucky, they send you back to Sudan.

Although the border between Egypt and Israel is guarded and in most places has three rolled, barbed wire fences, it is more porous than one might think, considering Israel's reputation for tight security. The local Bedouin were already conducting successful smuggling operations of cigarettes, drugs and prostitutes through the rugged desert and across the frontier.

Our Bedouin guides encouraged us, 'Be strong and be calm. Your only problem is here on the Egyptian side. If you reach Israel, you'll be okay. The Israeli soldiers will help you. They'll treat you with respect. Maybe then your life will be okay. We can't go with you to the fence, because when they see us, they'll shoot. Don't turn around. Always go forward. Because if you turn back, you'll lose your way and might be shot.' And with that the Bedouins ran away and left us.

The fence was still about 700 to 800 meters away. And the Egyptian soldiers were in between. I told my friend that we should hide ourselves. 'We'll creep along the ground until we reach the fence.'

It was very hard work. We were both afraid, but my friend was petrified. When we came near the fence the Egyptian police saw us from afar. They began shouting at us, but didn't see us clearly because it was still dark. We probably looked like small trees to them.

The Bedouins had told us, 'If they see you, just run.' My friend took that concept and bolted. It was a terrible risk. They couldn't see us properly, but as we ran they could tell we were Sudanese. Soldiers were running after us and shooting. I ran back and hid myself. It was daybreak, about 4 A.M. I remember being very, very tired.

My friend was caught. He was really crying, sobbing. And they kept beating him. I took a chance—with the help of what seemed to be a supernatural power—and jumped over the fence. I fell into the Israeli side where I lay unconscious.

When I awoke, the sun was bright. I went to the road and waited until I was found by Israeli soldiers. They took me to their camp. That was on June 22, 2006. They asked a lot of questions, but didn't make me feel I was their enemy, though Sudan has no diplomatic relations with Israel. They understood.

The soldiers gave me and other refugees food, but in our exhaustion we couldn't even eat. A doctor examined us, cleaning the wounds of one injured Darfurian and giving him medicine. In the evening we were taken to Negev Prison where we met about one hundred Africans living in tents inside the prison compound. The refugees were on one side and the Palestinian prisoners were on the other side.

Just before hearing Gabriel's story, we had eaten a tasty, filling meal. In a few hours we'd go to sleep in our comfortable beds. All around us were friends and people who loved us. But here was a man, a follower of God as we were, yet because he happened to be born in Sudan, his life had gone in a direction completely opposite to ours. I grew up in a loving, Jewish family in the U.S. and by choice I now lived in Israel, happily married with four children.

Life in prison wasn't that good. We had enough food. But we didn't understand why someone who had run away from war was being held in prison. The guards were kind and kept telling us, 'Don't worry. No one will beat you here.' They encouraged us to be patient.

I could only imagine other prisons Gabriel had been in where he obviously had been starved and beaten.

That's how it was in that prison. The only bad thing was that if we were sick, they wouldn't treat us because we weren't officially convicted prisoners. They told us, 'You haven't yet been sentenced in court, so we can only give you first aid, not medical care.'

We were moved from one prison to another, and after nearly a year I was released. In May 2007 I came to Eilat, but we were freed on condition. I am allowed to work in the Royal Beach Hotel in Eilat but cannot leave my job without permission. I'm concerned because the Israeli government threatens to deport us back to Egypt, and we're tired of living with that uncertainty.

When Gabriel stopped speaking, we were all speechless. How can he sit here and in such an emotionless voice tell us this?

I thought about the books I'd read and movies I'd seen about Holocaust survivors, and about friends of ours who had jumped off trains on the way to Auschwitz, crawled through tunnels out of the Warsaw Ghetto, or risked their lives working for the Underground during World War II. Hearing them, I was always in awe and when I tried to picture myself having their courage, I simply couldn't. Now I was in the presence of a man who had been persecuted because of his skin color and had recently endangered his life to find the kind of freedom that I enjoyed on a daily basis.

Gabriel's situation perplexed me. Freed on condition? Not allowed to leave Eilat? I wanted to better understand the predicament he and the other refugees faced. I'd read in the newspaper that the Israeli government planned to send them back to Egypt. Didn't they realize that Gabriel couldn't go back? He left Egypt because his life had been in danger, and now, having come to Israel, he'd be seen as a traitor if he returned to Egypt or Sudan.

Gabriel's talk was meant to prepare us to interact with the children on our "Fun Day" the next day. I would no longer see the Sudanese simply as people with black skin or as refugees in a general sort of way, but as brave, traumatized individuals. I understood that each adult and child had traveled a long distance—up the Nile from Sudan to Egypt, before making the perilous passage into Israel. How far they had journeyed emotionally and culturally, I had no idea.

I wondered how the children would respond to us. Would we notice the upheavals they'd experienced or would they act like "normal" children? Was this the beginning of a new chapter in our lives or a one-time event? The anticipation I felt was like opening a door and not knowing what mysteries waited on the other side.

Fun Day

The first time I saw Gabriel, he walked into the Shelter Hostel on a Friday evening with four friends, all of them tall, thin and extremely black. Joshua, our oldest son, is 6'3" (188cm)—but

Gabriel was even taller, probably 6'4" or 6'5". He had a receding hairline with a neat, trim haircut, and his short beard added to his distinguished appearance. Many people coming into the hostel are dressed as if they just came in from the beach, and in fact they may have, as this is a beach resort area. Gabriel, on the other hand, had on black slacks and a clean, white brand-name T-shirt. No flip-flops or sandals for Gabriel either, but dressy leather sandals.

I happened to be standing near the entrance to welcome those who came to our Friday night meeting.

"I'm Gabriel," he introduced himself. He spoke in surprisingly fluent English with an unrecognizable accent, as he reached out his hand. "So glad to meet you." Gabriel spoke thoughtfully, deliberately, and though I didn't yet know his story, I detected a hint of sadness in his voice.

"Me too," I said. "John told me about you." My husband had met him on a previous visit to our hostel.

Gabriel and his friends sat down on the back bench, towering above the dozen construction workers from mainland China who sat in front of them.

Questions began popping up in my mind. *How did you get to Israel? What are you doing here?*

But at that moment there was no time to talk. We were about to begin our usual Shabbat evening meeting. When we opened the Shelter in 1984 we aimed to create an oasis where people from all backgrounds could come and find spiritual, emotional and physical rest. We envisioned a hostel where backpackers could find inexpensive accommodation in a friendly atmosphere. But through the years it had become much more than that—a vibrant community and a home away from home for thousands. Guests from every continent, background and religion stay for one night or for years, while other people just drop by for a cup of coffee or a chat.

The Friday that Gabriel appeared, over one hundred people from all corners of the globe had gathered together as usual— crowded into the courtyard under the quickly darkening sky. Throughout the week, the 30-by-10 meter (300 by 100 feet) courtyard boasted a bench swing, a few lounge chairs and a raised platform at one end covered with rugs and mattresses. At the other end the succah (hut) has a palm frond roof supported by palm trunks. Furnished with old sofas and rugs, it is our outdoor lounge area. This is where the staff and others who want to join us, meet every morning at 11:00 after cleaning the hostel, to sing songs and read a portion of the Bible.

But on Fridays, white plastic chairs fill the area and those who don't find a place to sit often stand in the back. Two strings of light bulbs are roped from one end to the other.

I made my way to the front, picked up my guitar and we began singing—first in English and Hebrew, followed by Russian, Spanish and Chinese, representing the main groups participating in this unique gathering. A projector connected to a laptop flashed the words to the songs on the white wall as the Russians, Hispanics and Chinese stood up in turn to sing. Some people were present for the first time, while others had been coming weekly for years. The Russians were in fact new immigrants in Israel coming from countries making up the former Soviet Union, while the Spanish speakers had immigrated from Cuba, Argentina, Mexico, Peru, Columbia and other lands.

In a short message from the Bible, John focused on the necessity of starting a new, spiritual life, his words being simultaneously translated into four languages. The various language groups sat together with an interpreter in front of each section. (Visitors occasionally complain about the noise or chaos and say it's hard for them to concentrate on their own language. I prefer to view it as a preview of heaven when all tribes and languages and peoples will be gathered together as one.)

John compared the Sudanese refugees' journey from Egypt into Israel with the children of Israel's exodus from the bondage of slavery into the Promised Land. And throughout his talk I couldn't take my eyes off our five Sudanese visitors.

After the meeting, as everyone shared a meal of vegetable soup, rice, lentil stew and coleslaw, Gabriel spoke to some of our Chinese friends with the help of an interpreter from Hong Kong.

"Where are you from?" one of the Chinese construction

workers asked, bending his head back to talk to the tall Sudanese man. "What brought you here?"

Gabriel offered a short explanation, and I was impressed by his quiet, patient manner. "Finally I feel at home," he finished.

In the balmy May evening, no one was in a hurry to go home and the camaraderie continued later than usual. Finally, with the chairs stacked, floor swept, dishes washed, and quietness reigning once more, I was left wondering where this encounter with Gabriel would lead.

We had read in the newspapers about a new phenomenon in Israel—refugees from Africa crossing the Egyptian border. John had been following the news of the refugees in the media and was eager to locate those in need and to help them in any way he could. Since landing in South Africa in 1964 as an eighteen-year-old cook in the Dutch merchant marine, John had a heart for the downtrodden of the earth. He was enraged when he saw poor black people with tin cans coming to the docks and begging for food from the ship and then being kicked away. This passion never left him, though as he matured he found better ways to help than to enter into fistfights on behalf of the oppressed.

God has a special love for strangers, as is written in Deuteronomy 10:18-19: "The Lord defends the cause of the fatherless and the widow and loves the alien, giving him food and clothing. And you are to love those who are aliens, for you yourselves were aliens in Egypt." We felt that since God loves foreigners and refugees, then shouldn't we also?

Mansur, who worked at the Shelter Hostel, heard that many Sudanese were staying at the Red Rock Hotel, the housing for the workers from Club Hotel, one of the largest hotels in Eilat. Mansur, an Israeli from a Druze background, had a big advantage over the rest of us as an Arabic speaker who could converse with the Arab-speaking Sudanese. He started to go regularly to the hotel to play with the children. One thing led to another until Mansur and several friends decided to treat the Sudanese children to the most fun day of their lives. He invited Gabriel to help.

In the morning of the big day, the event planners divided into

two teams. One team bought each of the forty children a new
pair of sandals. Many of them had arrived in Israel barefoot. Then
they took the children to visit Eilat's Underwater Observatory,
the aquarium where visitors can watch the fish swimming in their
own environment. Meanwhile, the second team was at our house
cooking lunch for everyone.

My first encounter with the children was when we all met
together on the beach to eat. There were big children, little ones,
babies and mothers. We chose a sandy beach with large areas of
shade provided by white parachute material. Plastic chairs and
picnic tables were also available free of charge.

Most western children would probably begin playing in the
sand, looking for sea shells or the pretty rocks and pieces of coral
that characterize the Red Sea beaches. These Sudanese children of
all ages just looked stunned as if they didn't know what to do.

"Sit down on chairs in a circle!" Mansur directed them in
Arabic. It took a while but finally most of them caught on to the
principle. "Okay, quiet! Let's thank God for the food."

Some began attacking their food; others just stared. I thought
that maybe they weren't used to schnitzels and pitas and
hummus. Much of the food was falling to the ground or was
thrown away.

"Pick up the cups and leftovers off the sand," I said, trying
to explain with hand motions. I've always been a stickler for
not wasting food or littering. The beach was busy and we were
drawing lots of attention. Forty black children were an unusual
sight on the crowded beach. I certainly didn't want to leave a
mess behind.

An Israeli woman was seated near us with her own two little
girls. She came up to us. "Who are these children? Where are
they from?"

"They're refugees from Sudan." John answered proudly,
already beginning to feel protective of his new charges.

"I'd like to buy them all popsicles," the woman offered.

When we finally took the children into the water, we were
thankful to have plenty of adults along with air mattresses,

because those wild kids obviously didn't know how to swim. But what excitement!

I looked at each child, at each happy face. What had they been through? Those mothers sitting in the shade with their babies—were they as young as they looked? What about fathers—were they in the picture?

Some of the guys organized a football game. The kids loved it, even if they didn't always seem to be actually playing on teams. One little boy was running with his pants pulled down to his knees, peeing as he ran. He didn't want to miss a minute of the fun.

Many questions arose. Playing with the children and giving them a good time was easy. But was there a way to reach out to the adults, most of whom didn't speak English? What about making a long-term difference? Could we really make an impact in their lives?

At the end of the day Gabriel came up to me. "This has been the best day of my whole life," he said in all seriousness.

This? I thought. The Observatory, a picnic on the beach, and swimming? At age thirty?

A Family of Paramount Chiefs

*H*earing bits of Gabriel's story whetted my appetite to know more. The opportunity arose when Gabriel had to go to Jerusalem for a check-up at Hadassah Hospital. He felt pain in his liver and John offered to drive him.

"We'll be together in the car for four hours," I told John. "What do you think if I record Gabriel's story? Then I can transfer it onto our computer. After that, we'll see what we can do with it."

"That's a good idea," John said, "if Gabriel agrees."

Sitting in the back seat of our car, as we took the four-and-a-half hour drive to Jerusalem, Gabriel held the small tape recorder in his hand and began speaking:

I'm Gabriel Thon Kuol Mading, a Sudanese from the south and a Dinka by tribe. I'm from Jonglei State, from the town of Bor. Some people say it's called Bor because, during the rainy season, that area is always flooded by waters from the River Nile, and a flood is called Abor.

In Bor and in Jonglei State there are many tribes. Most of the Dinka people are on the other side of the River Nile, in the state of Bahr el Ghazal. Bahr means river. And Ghazal means gazelle because there were once many gazelles living in the area. But portions of Dinka are called Bor, and I'm from a village called Panpiol, where my grandfather was a paramount chief.

We do not know where our ancestors came from. Some believe that we were created out of the river. The River Nile is important to us—for the cattle to graze, for us to drink, and for farming. Our grandfathers struggled and fought each other to defend the area.

That's where I was born. At the time, Bor was very small. Except for several modern homes, most of the houses were constructed of grass thatch. My father, as a council employee, had one large house given to him by the government, but outside of town there were many traditional huts plus a big one for the cattle. Bor had a few schools, some offices, a prison and a hospital. Our town had only a few cars and trucks but there were many bicycles. The bicycles were for adults, but older kids also rode them even though they couldn't sit when they pedaled.

Bor is right on the banks of the Nile, so in the rainy season it was really green with many trees, bushes and flowers. Fields of corn, millet and peanuts, and orchards of fruit trees surrounded us. We grew bananas, not commercially, but for subsistence, and we had mangos, papayas and lemons. Okra and a kind of leafy green vegetable like chard, were our favorite vegetables.

Much of our food—milk, butter and cheese—came from our cows. Our main meal, kissera, was made from pounded grains mixed with water and wheat flour, and it looked like flat bread. Kissera is delicious to eat with soup made from vegetables and meat. Another common food was Ugali, a thick porridge of maize or other grains and flour. Millet flour was another traditional food, cooked and eaten with milk.

I was born to the family of Mading Majok, a paramount chief, who had many wives. Altogether he had twenty-something wives. I've seen twelve of them myself, including my grandmother, Akur. She had six children—two sons, two daughters, and two sons who died when they were young. In the tradition of our fathers, if your brother died, you had to marry an additional wife for him in order for your family to grow large. So my father and my uncle, who is now a paramount chief, each took one wife for their brothers who had died as children years before. It's something like the book of Ruth in the Bible when Boaz, the kinsman-redeemer married Ruth so that the name of her dead husband, Elimelech, would not be blotted out. Our enemies had a joke that Dinkas never die. If they killed a Dinka man, his brother, uncle or cousin could marry in his place and perpetuate his name.

I was born about thirty years ago, around 1978. I have to estimate because when someone is born in a village, it doesn't get recorded. On my passport someone just picked a date for my birthday and wrote May 6. Many Sudanese are given the birthday of January 1.

My father is one of the few Dinka people who went to school. He went up to grade four. I think he started school around the year 1930 because he must have been born around 1924. But he didn't know because he was from a village.

At that time Sudan was under British colonial rule in cooperation with the Egyptians. After grade four my father went two years to a teachers' training college and began teaching. He left the teaching profession to join the police. But in the same year, 1956, as he was training to be a police officer, the first civil war broke out between the south and the north. We in the south are black Africans and mainly Christians and animists, while in the north, they are Arab Muslims.

We received our independence from Britain in 1956. And we immediately revolted—the south against the north. Britain's policy had been that we couldn't share the country with the Arabs. They knew we'd have problems and could never agree on issues such as religion, economy and politics. Since the British left and Sudan gained independence in 1956, there has been little stability and peace in Sudan.

*A*s I listened I realized that Sudan's independence came a few years after the creation of the state of Israel in 1948. Within days of Israel's declaration of independence, a major war broke out when five Arab nations invaded Israel. Over 6,000 Israelis lost their lives. In subsequent wars many more soldiers and civilians were killed. Since I immigrated to Israel in 1976, I've experienced the first and second wars with Lebanon. But through it all, our lives continued on. Those who lost loved ones or temporarily had to leave their homes suffered immeasurably, but no one lost their whole family, had their entire village or town eliminated, or saw their country reduced to ruins as in Sudan.

*G*reat Britain told us at that time, 'You southerners, we know you cannot live together with Arabs. Your culture is different. Your beliefs are different. But if you reject our advice, it's up to you to figure it out.' Their aim was to separate us. Southern Sudan could become part of Uganda. But that didn't happen.

The Arabs were cunning and clever. They persuaded our tribal leaders—we had no educated people at that time—saying, 'All we Sudanese are friends. We're all Africans. Compared to the whites, we share almost the same culture. The British are different. They've been looting our country so let's fight them together.'

Our grandparents, through their ignorance, accepted. But the war between the north and south continued. Self-rule however, never materialized. It didn't work at all. The Arabs never accepted us and instead became our foes. They said that they couldn't share the rule with non-worshipers, non-Muslims.

At that time most of our people were animists. They didn't believe as I believe now, in Christianity. They followed the spirit of our ancestors. In our village, my ancestors worshipped a snake the color of army clothes with black spots. They called it Atem. I think in English it's called a python and it's very poisonous. Even today many people are called Atem, like the snake. That's the name of our common ancestor, our great-great-grandfather. But even as they worshipped it, Atem slithered around in nearly every house.

It was taboo to kill the snake. If you killed it, old people would bury the snake as they bury people. They believed that when the full moon came again, Atem would resurrect. Sometimes the snake didn't touch or hurt anyone. But if Atem did bite someone and they died, people would say, 'They must have done something wrong.' Or, 'They didn't bring a cow for their daughter's dowry.'

In our village we had a medium, a man who pretended to talk secretly to Atem. If there was a problem in the village, people came to him and asked, 'Can you consult Atem?' It could have been a drought, a cattle disease or an attack by other tribes. They made the snake the master of the village. Today we ask the Lord because we know only God has power. But they trusted in Atem. They knew there was a Creator God but the snake was the small god who could solve their problems.

These days the snakes have disappeared and it's rare to find them any more. At times you might see them in the bush.

Gabriel's explanation of his ancestors' snake worship sounded incongruous, knowing his deep faith in God and the Bible. I tried to imagine just a generation ago his people praying to a snake in times of difficulty. Today Gabriel expresses gratitude to God for liberating him from the bondage of frightening superstitions, and he smiles as he remembers his ancestors' beliefs.

My father left the police force and began working in Bor's local council as a storekeeper. I found out later that, from 1956 until the terrible war broke out in 1983, my father controlled all the stores of fuel and other supplies in our area. He was highly trusted.

I'm from the line of chieftains. I can date back about eleven ancestors from my grandfather. Atemdemkeer was our first grandfather. Now my uncle is chief.

In our culture, your importance was based on your cattle and your wives. My father inherited a lot of cattle from his grandparents. And during the time he worked in the local council, he bought more cows. My father had seven wives. Although he was a Christian, he was still influenced by the Dinka traditions. His name was Kuol Mading because his father was Mading, and his baptism name was Lazarus.

We Dinka are mostly very tall, but my father wasn't as tall as his brothers. They were mostly 190 to 195 cm (6'3" to 6' 5") and one was even 2 meters (6'7") tall. My father was a strong man though. He always wore a suit and dressed sharply. I have a small photo of him that one of my relatives in Egypt gave me.

My mother was his third wife and she had seven children. She was taller than my father and she was slim. She wasn't educated, so she didn't dress like those in the town, but her clothes weren't completely traditional like the villagers either. I really liked her cooking—the way she prepared traditional food and also modern food. She used our traditional way of making butter: milking the cows, putting the cream in a gourd, and letting it sit for six or seven hours. Then she would shake the gourd, pounding it on her lap until the butter was formed.

Gabriel stopped speaking and mimed the butter-making process, putting his hands together and lifting them up and down in front of his face in the direction of his folded legs. He smiled. Was he remembering his mother's delicious cooking? I thought about some favorite dishes my mother used to prepare. I liked her brisket, chopped liver, spaghetti sauce, cheese cake, and stuffing for turkey. Before my thoughts drifted further, Gabriel returned to the story of his family:

I'm number five. First there were three daughters followed by a son, then me, then another brother, and last came another girl.

We inherit our names from our ancestors. We would be named after a grandfather, grandmother or a cow. When a man married a wife, he paid cows to his in-laws—maybe thirty or fifty—and the rich could even offer one hundred fifty cows. So when he gave the dowry to his wife's relatives, later he would name some of his children after the cows he had given.

Our children receive names based on our cattle, especially the most beautiful cow among them. A girl will get the name of a female cow; a boy will get the name of a bull. All the cows have names. The female cows have special names, usually relating to their color. The females receive their names when they give birth for the first time. It might be called by the name of the cattle camp where it gave birth. Or if you get a cow from an uncle or another relative, you call the cow by the name of that uncle. I inherited the name of Thon, a beautiful, white bull, so I could be called Mabior, meaning 'white,' or else just Thon.

One sister was called Ajok. She received her name from one of the beautiful white cows with black around its eyes and on its back. My oldest sister was called Aluel, the name of a cow but also the name of our great-grandmother.

In my tribe I'm called Thon Kuol Mading Majok Anyang after the name of the bull given to my mother's relatives as a dowry. Gabriel is my Christian name.

My brother Majuk received the name of the father of Mading, the chief. My brother was very active and violent, quarreling with our brother Abiew all the time because they were close in age. But I only remember fighting with him twice because I didn't like to argue and he knew not to provoke me. But he could also be really friendly. I guess we were like any brothers—fighting and playing.

The one who follows me is called Mading, the name of my paternal grandfather. And the last one is Akur.

I remember my two oldest sisters as loving and quiet. They

weren't living with us all the time because they went to school in another town. But when they were home they helped my mother, especially taking care of the rest of us.

Among my siblings, I know the whereabouts of only two sisters, one in Australia and the other in Kenya. I heard my brothers are in south Sudan. I heard my mother is in Bor, but I'm not sure. My father died.

That is the story of my family. We were a respected family.

All those names, paramount chiefs and generations! And the meanings of their names! I guess that part shouldn't be so strange to me. In Hebrew, our names have meanings too, which we usually take into account when we name our children. But to name your child after a cow?!

When I lived in Alaska years ago I discovered that the old cliché is true—Eskimos have many different words for "snow." Now I was finding that the Dinkas seem to have many different ways of describing cows and the colors of cows.

I couldn't follow all of Gabriel's descriptions of the names of his sisters and brothers, or the connections with all their ancestors. But I was touched as he explained everything in such detail. Maybe reciting this was a way for him to memorialize all those people he had lost, even those who he believed to be alive but had vanished from his life. Still, I couldn't fully comprehend.

Running

We were driving north through the Arava Valley. Communal settlements—kibbutzim and moshavim—popped up periodically, surrounded by date plantations, greenhouses and emerald-green fields. I wondered if the dry plains studded with acacia trees reminded Gabriel of landscapes in Africa. Though from what I had heard, south Sudan was green and fertile. How did Gabriel

feel seeing Israel turning the wilderness into gardens? I felt I
was seeing familiar sights through new eyes. Gabriel continued
speaking without a pause.

During the war that broke out in 1956 my uncle, Mayen
Mading, was assassinated. He had become the paramount chief
after my grandfather died. The Arab leader accused him of helping
the anti-government rebels. So in 1968, in our small village of
about 4,000 residents, he was caught by the Arabs along with 38
sub-chiefs—a terrible slaughter.

Mayen Mading and the other southerners were hung on a
bamboo tree, a death you could compare to that of our Lord Jesus.
To get information about the rebels, they put nails in their heads,
pressed and tightened them, and tortured them to death. If you
were a coward and broke down, you would talk a lot and provide
them with the facts they sought.

After my uncle and those sub-chiefs died, the Arabs put them
in a dry well, poured petrol on them, and burned them, so they
couldn't even be buried. No one in Sudan truly understood what
happened in 1968 with the death of the Dinka chiefs in the south.
They were killed protecting their land, defending their dignity. My
uncle left behind ten wives.

I was about six years old when war came to our area in 1983.

John Garang, a highly educated Dinka who inspired the war,
was also from Bor, from our area of Twic. He rose in the
Sudanese Armed Forces to the rank of colonel. In the first war,
from 1956 to 1972, he was one of the fighters of Anyanya 1, the
rebel movement that was fighting for the liberation of the south.
I'm not sure what that name means. Afterwards Garang went
to Tanzania where he studied agriculture. After they signed the
agreement to end the 17-year war, he was sent by the government
to the United States where he obtained his Ph.D.

The agreement was signed in 1972, but the conditions of the
agreement weren't honored. Most of those who signed the agreement were disappointed and the common people were unhappy.

The army wanted to transfer one of the battalions of Anyanya from Bor to the north, undermining their power. They wanted to dissolve the former rebel militia so the government would have complete control. But the southern battalion wasn't willing to move because then they would be integrated into the regular Sudanese army. Their refusal was the beginning of the rebel movement that afterwards came to be known as the Sudanese People's Liberation Army, or SPLA.

The government army called in reinforcements to attack the battalion's garrison. The rebels would probably not call it a defeat, but in fact they were forced to run away and regroup. John Garang fled to Ethiopia.

*H*ere Gabriel laughed, and I wondered what was so funny about John Garang running away? As I waited and listened, Gabriel soon answered my question.

*T*he way it occurred was actually funny. John Garang was an officer in the Sudanese Armed Forces. Hearing about the rebellion brewing, the army's leaders were worried. So the government sent Garang to Bor telling him to calm the rebellion, which was led by Major Keruvino who happened to be a colleague of Garang's in Anyanya. Instead, Garang encouraged the rebels and joined them. That's when he left for Ethiopia.

When the rebel forces ran away to the bush, most of the civil servants ran with them. They ran through our area, heading north before turning east to Ethiopia where Garang started his revolution. Many people followed him. But my father wasn't willing to leave because he was aging and knew he'd be caught.

He told our family, 'If I go to the bush with the rebels and come back later, I will be accused of joining the opposition and be killed.' So he remained in town.

At that time my father was staying in his council house and my mother and we children were in the house near the cattle camp with some cows. My father knew what would happen and being a civil servant, he tried to hire a car to take us to our ancestral village where we'd be safe, but he failed.

When the rebellion started early in the morning on May 16, I was home with my mother, brothers, sisters and cows. We all were confused about where to go. In the chaos, my mother ran with the other villagers and I went with my uncle. Being the first time I was away from my mom, I felt lost and miserable. My uncle knew the area so he helped and encouraged me. Even though danger surrounded us, we moved slowly because we were with our animals. But everyone had rushed in the same general direction and some days later I was reunited again with my mother.

I grew exhausted from all that walking and I remember being terribly thirsty. We left everything—including blankets and food—except a little milk and meat. Once in a while we would kill a cow and then we'd eat it together with other people because we couldn't keep the meat fresh.

At least I had my mother and she was serious about taking care of me. I suffered from local diseases like malaria and yellow fever. When malaria attacks you the first time, you shiver and after some minutes you start vomiting and have a fever. It kills many people, especially children. We had no medicine except the traditional kind—roots and other things—which may or may not help.

The fighting was intense at that time. The government was attacking us and bombing our cattle. They pounded our area with the Antonov, a Russian-made and dangerous aircraft. Because most of our cattle are white, they could see our large cattle camps from the air. And where they see cows, they know there are people close by.

'Run! Hide!' my mother would scream at me when we heard that loud droning sound approaching. 'Don't worry about the cows!'

When the bombs dropped you could hear a lot of mothers, each one yelling to her children. Many people were killed.

It took us some days to get from the town to the village because of our cattle. It was one of the first times I left home and went to the cattle camp, because normally we kept our cows near our house. It took about a week for us to reach our ancestral village. Although I was little, I realized the danger from the sound of the shooting and guns. When you heard the Antonovs overhead, you either became paralyzed in fear, or you went charging around like crazy.

So the killing was going on in the south—destruction against civilians without discrimination. By the time I was only five years old, even before I fled, I'd already seen a lot of people killed.

My half-brothers and sisters sped to the bush. Some of my brothers were fifteen and didn't want to be caught. They were hurrying toward Ethiopia because we'd heard that if you didn't die on the way, the United Nations there might take care of you. And the strong ones could join the rebels and come back to Sudan and fight. Some of my brothers enlisted.

I was in the area of Bor with my mother, wondering where my house and my cows were, wandering from place to place. We couldn't stay in one place. The government used to loot our cows—my father had many. We hid in the bush with some of the cows. My uncles or distant relatives kept others.

Warnings and rumors circulated constantly. 'Don't go to that place! The government took some boys from there.' That's what interested them—taking boys. So we'd run to another place with our elders. But those whom we looked up to couldn't really protect us or else they'd be killed for it.

My mother tried to comfort me. 'Don't worry,' she said. 'We'll be fine. We have a lot of milk and grain and we're still farming.'

Our area was good for cultivation, with different types of millet being the main crop. We grew lots of sesame too. Our fear, though, was that the government would come, kidnap us, and take the cows. We were tired of fleeing from place to place.

From 1983 to 1987 our life was stressful. Food was no problem, but when the government heard that rebels were in a particular place, they would come and even abduct children. So in 1987 when I was about ten years old, I decided to run away and join the other boys who were fleeing our area.

Our only goal for the future was to reach Ethiopia where we
hoped we would be safe. So we headed toward Ethiopia.

When we left, we knew our situation was hopeless. The
distance itself was very far. If we weren't killed by the Arabs,
we'd die of hunger or thirst, or be attacked by wild animals—lions,
leopards and hyenas, although we didn't fear the hyenas so much.
Crocodiles and hippos, though, are extremely dangerous and lurk
in the many rivers we had to cross.

My mother was really desperate but there was no way she
could protect me. We had no other option than for me to leave
with the other boys.

As the mother of four children I couldn't imagine sending my
ten-year-old son away on a dangerous trek with little hope of
survival. Yet this sacrifice by Sudanese mothers is similar to what
many Jewish mothers in Germany, Poland, Holland and other
countries did to save their children from the Nazis in World War
II. Mothers handed their sons and daughters and even babies over
to strangers hoping to preserve their lives.

I left in the winter when there's no rain in Sudan. The
rainy season begins in April and continues until November. When
there's enough rain, people are happy.

The dry season, December to March, is very hot. During
that time everything withers and shrivels—people, animals, crops
and the earth. Just before the rain falls, strong winds blow and
leaves drop from the trees. Clouds begin to form and the heat is
suffocating. Even with the first showers of rain, it's still sizzling.

Those are our two seasons.

Our elders encouraged us, 'Our children, we have no way to
help you. You must go. Maybe God will take care of you.'

They knew that many of us would not come back, but perhaps
a few might live.

My village is situated in the middle of the bend of the River

Nile. Many Dinka boys from destroyed areas on the other side of the river—from Bahr el Ghazal State—were coming through alone. Having walked for almost two months already, some of these 'Lost Boys' were dying before our eyes.

'The boys were out herding cattle and became separated from their families when the bombing began,' I've heard it explained. But I knew there was another reason.

During the war the policy of the Arab-controlled government was to Islamize the boys especially. They aimed to change our ideology. The government soldiers might seize girls and women and abuse them, but boys were crucial to their plan to create a new Muslim society. They would completely brainwash the boys, give them guns, and send them back to kill their own people. That's how they operated. And that's why our parents sent us boys away.

We joined those other Dinka boys and together took another month to reach Ethiopia.

On the way we were attacked by other tribes who opposed the Dinka. Because of the assaults, the few rebel soldiers traveling with us spent time securing each place before we advanced. Some of them had broken away from the government army and were on their way to join the south Sudanese forces in Ethiopia. They didn't even have bullets but hoped to scare our assailants with their guns.

Most of the rebels fighting the government were from Dinka tribes. It's a tradition of southern Sudanese that we battle other tribes. So at this time, those other tribes, even those who had been our friends, were incited against us by the government. They were told, 'You have to fight and kill the Dinka.'

There's a small tribe called Murle to the east of Bor. Although they are our friends, we have a traditional war with them. They have a sexually-transmitted disease called Syphilis, which can be passed on to their babies, causing stillbirths or newborn deaths. A Murle woman is lucky to have even one or two living children.

With the Dinka there's more control and accountability. Messing up is not common traditionally. If you commit adultery, you'll be either fined, have to pay a lot of cows, or even be killed. But in Murle there's no control. Many men will go to one woman. So they have many diseases. For this reason they kidnap Dinka children, young girls and boys, and adopt them as their own.

As we were going through that area, it was really a very, very hard time. Many children were grabbed by that tribe. They took them, changed the traditions they had grown up with, and put traditional Murle scars on them.

Our leaders told us, 'After 5 P.M. no child should move around outside. Those Murle may be hiding between the trees and come and snatch you.'

For us children that was frightening! We'd already left our village and lost our parents. We certainly didn't want to lose our tribal identity as well.

We Dinka maintain our principles. We pride ourselves on not taking other people's things. All our cows were our own, unlike other Nilotic tribes (ethnic groups from the Nile basin) who believe that any cows they see are theirs. Yet as we journeyed, other tribes were attacking us, taking children, and stealing cows.

Our response was just to defend ourselves. Even if we defeated them in a fight, we would never seize their children. We might take their cows but never their children. We couldn't kill their children because it was taboo—children and women aren't to be killed.

Dinka Rituals

As Dinka we maintain certain cultural rituals. When you reach a certain age, your lower teeth are removed. You could be as young as eight years old, or as old as fifteen. This is our initiation into manhood. You won't be a boy anymore; you're joining the men. And along with having your teeth removed, your forehead would be cut with a sharp knife to produce the ritual scars. In most Dinka clans, the ceremony includes making those marks, except among us from Bor.

I had noticed the straight lines of scars on many of our Sudanese friends' foreheads as well as their missing bottom teeth. In the beginning I found this look strange, if not gruesome. But to my surprise I became used to their appearance and as time went on I felt I could even understand the scars' attractiveness. The knocked out teeth disturbed me more. I've always placed a high value on proper mouth hygiene, perhaps because my father is a dentist. And it seems like it would be difficult to chew with a big gap in their bite.

*F*or our initiation they put a group of one or two hundred of us boys and girls in a separate place or house. We were taught by the elders and kept apart for about three months.

I'll never forget my six lower front teeth being gouged out with a piece of iron. It is done by those who are knowledgeable. They say you won't feel it since you're young, but it's extremely painful. Even today when I hear the sound of two pieces of iron grinding, I feel it in the nerves in my head—a sound like 'cling.'

Before the ritual begins, the elders give you words of encouragement. If you're brave you sit alone. They praise you and say, 'This is a strong young boy.' If you're afraid, they grab you and hold you down.

Later, when you're older, you definitely don't want girls to call you a coward. Nor do you want your age mates to mock and remind you, 'You cried when they removed your teeth. You had to be held down.'

You would be ashamed. So you have to be brave.

There's a lot of blood and it takes almost a month to heal. For about three days you don't eat solid foods—only warm milk and then porridge till you're okay. For the first week, if you eat something you don't really taste it. After two weeks your taste comes back. It's very painful. We did it with boys and girls together, though sometimes the girls are in a separate place.

Removing teeth is dangerous because they use the same knife on everyone and can pass diseases. So today the process is being discouraged, although some people still follow that tradition. I don't think I'd have false teeth made even if someone would offer to do it for free. But I don't believe young people should follow this ritual anymore.

Books about the "Lost Boys" who were resettled in America tell that some have had teeth implants to replace those knocked out in their initiation rites. A number of Sudanese have asked John if he could arrange implants for them. We've helped them with many medical issues, but new teeth have been beyond our budget.

We Dinka are one tribe composed of different clans. Our dialects are diverse as well as the pattern of marks. For example, my Dinka friends from Bahr el Ghazal cut five or six scars on the forehead. Others cut all around, although it also depends on the shape of your head. We can recognize someone's clan by the marks. During the war the scars were dangerous because they easily identified you and you could be killed by other tribes or by the Arabs.

Our marks are not compulsory. They're a decoration—up to you if you want them. No one would force you. I didn't want the scars. Some people in our area did it because they thought it made them more attractive. Knocking out the teeth hurts more. With the marks it is possible for them to accidentally cut the veins and that is agonizing. But our clan's marks aren't very painful because they're small and don't reach into the skull. It's just a double V and takes only a few seconds to cut.

Removing the teeth and cutting the marks is an important tradition for us Dinka. Our elders used to say to us, 'Now you are grown up. You will do the hard work now. You won't milk the cows anymore—that's women's work. And you shouldn't be around the kitchen—it's for mothers and their daughters. You must respect the women but not mix with them. Your sisters will bring food to you.

'The fathers will teach you our traditions. You will help your father in the field and with cutting firewood. You will search for the cows when they're lost and care for them, especially the calves. When you take the cows outside, you have to be ready to defend them from lions, even if you're only eleven or twelve.

'When you grow up, you will defend our land as our fathers did. At first you will help from behind, not yet in the front line. Now you will be with the boys and the fathers.'

In my case, I was forced to run away from my home right after the ceremony. That's the reason I did it at that time. If I came back after the war with my teeth, my age mates would laugh at me. They would never respect someone who still had his lower teeth, but would say, 'What do you know about our culture or way of life? What can you tell us?' That's how it is in our village.

If your father had a lot of cows, you took up a spear in his honor and killed a cow. You gave the meat to others, not eating it yourself. So in 1986, when I was about ten years old, I killed a cow. It's a great privilege because it shows you're rich. Not everyone owned cows and someone with only a few might not want to kill them.

After that you received another name. They might call you, 'The Man Who Killed Ten Cows' or something like that. My new name was 'Amor,' the name of the cow that was killed and eaten for my initiation party. Other people ate the cow, but I didn't eat it because it was killed in honor of me. So those are our traditions of passing from the boy-state to the man-state. You've changed and now belong with the big people.

God Knows Our Suffering

*F*aces of "our boys" flashed before me—Yohannes, Dongdiet, Ryan, Peter and their friends—young, eager, coal-black and bright-eyed. When he began his hopeless journey, Gabriel was even younger than they are.

Our boys were young teenagers who had crossed the border

from Egypt to Israel at night under fire from Egyptian soldiers. But at least one parent had accompanied nearly all of them.

Once, when we took them for a hike in the mountains outside Eilat, I asked them about their passage. Walking in the rough rocky hills, I wondered if memories would flood back to them of that dark crossing. (Thanks to their schooling in Egypt, the boys speak passable English.)

"Yeah, we had to hide and then run, and then we were in Israel," Dongdiet told me. Outwardly they didn't seem to be affected by a return to the mountains.

I wondered, was that nightmare so easily forgotten because now they felt safe? Or was I just missing the message because of the language barrier or their shyness?

The Israeli soldiers stationed near the border that Saturday morning certainly took the boys' presence seriously. When they saw us stepping out of our car with six Sudanese boys, four soldiers raced down the hill.

"Who are these boys?" the officer asked. "What are you doing here?"

"We come hiking here a lot," John said. "These are my boys."

The soldiers looked at John as if he were crazy. One baby-faced soldier didn't take his finger off the trigger of his gun while glaring at us.

"Are you sure they're not trying to sneak into Israel?" he demanded.

"Look which direction we're coming from," John pointed out. "From Eilat. Not from Egypt. And look how well they're dressed. Do they look like they just crossed the border? Ask them something in Hebrew. Their parents work in hotels. They come by our house every day after school."

The officer, a woman, called for more reinforcements.

We waited.

Josh, our oldest son, was with us. He was visiting us for the weekend from Jerusalem where he had just begun working as a lawyer. "Listen," he said, "we've been here for nearly an hour. Isn't it obvious by now? Do we look like human traffickers or smugglers? And look at these young boys. They're undoubtedly traumatized after all their negative experiences with Egyptian police and soldiers on the border. We understand you have an important job to do, but do they deserve this treatment?"

Living in Israel, I was used to speaking to soldiers and understood the necessity of tight security. Our four children had all served in the Israeli army. But now, since meeting the Sudanese, I was seeing life through the eyes of the refugees.

I saw the fear on Johannes' face. At best, their situation in Israel was fragile. Was he wondering if the soldiers would try to detain them or send them back? The boys looked to us as their guardians and had implicit faith in us.

The soldiers were finally convinced and allowed us to continue on our way, to begin our hike.

I felt protective of these boys. Like the rest of the Sudanese in Eilat, they called John "Abuna" ("father"). Since arriving in Eilat, they would come to our house every afternoon. In the mornings they would go to a school for Sudanese children. But in the afternoons, because their parents worked long hours, the children would have a lot of unsupervised time, and they tended to roam around. Or maybe Sudanese parents just weren't used to interacting with their children as we do. Another one of those culture differences I couldn't quite grasp.

In any case, a group of about twenty boys adopted us as their hangout and came every day to our house and the Shelter. They managed to acquire bicycles, prized possessions, which they parked in our garden. Sometimes they just stopped by for a visit and a snack. We became attached to them; we felt it was an opportunity to have a positive impact at a crucial time in their lives.

What was their future? Would it be in Israel or some other country? Would the Israeli government agree to let the refugees remain or would they fulfill their threat to send the Sudanese back to Egypt or Sudan?

I imagined our boys walking from Sudan to Ethiopia as Gabriel had, being attacked by soldiers and lions, faced with

starvation and thirst. *Could they have survived?* I wondered as
Gabriel continued his story.

*N*ot all of us reached Ethiopia. We were protected by two or
three rebel neighbors who were guiding us and fighting for us.
But still, lions, leopards, and other wild animals killed many. Boys
also died of hunger and thirst. Some were shot. Although the tribal
militias were fighting with our guards, the bullets reached us too.

Each child received a tiny ration of water, barely enough for
one day. In the desert they weighed the precious water for us.

'Be strong,' our leaders told us. 'When you reach the river you
can drink as much as you want.'

Thankfully, in south Sudan a lot of gazelles pass through
in herds, and our leaders hunted them. We children collected
firewood and skinned and butchered the animals. We put the meat
right on the fire. We had only a few pots, so if another group was
cooking, we had to wait before we could have some soup. Only if
we stayed in one place for a few days, did we have time to wait.
Otherwise roasting was the main way to cook. There were also
wild vegetables to forage in the bush. We just ate what we wanted,
depending on where we came from and what kind of wild fruits we
had learned about in our area.

There were so many of us children traveling, that I can't even
estimate the number. In 1987 when we reached a place called
Panyido over the border in Ethiopia, there were more than twenty
thousand boys. For various reasons, no girls were with us.

Because most of us were young, even eight years old, we
started getting childhood diseases like chicken pox and measles. I
witnessed a lot of my cousins dying in the camp but I didn't catch
those sicknesses because I'd already had them at home. Many of
us died of hunger and diseases. There was no treatment. Our rebel
guards were trying to help us, but what could they do?

'You must come and care for these thousands of children,' the
Ethiopian government begged the United Nations.

They came; but still our life was very, very, very hard. We

suffered a lot. We were left to fend for ourselves. We had to build our own houses and construct roads too. When we went to the bush to fell trees, some of our friends never returned. We left them out there, killed by lions.

The few adults all lived separately from us. The grownups couldn't even help us except to just lend a hand in burying our friends. We buried most of them ourselves but if adults were around they helped us. They could also assist in unloading relief supplies from trucks, work that was too heavy for us boys.

*W*hat emotional scars do the boys carry after seeing their friends mangled by lions and burying others with their own hands? We sometimes question whether to take children to a relative's funeral, but Gabriel experienced death all around him.

*W*e were divided into about twenty units, each one with a thousand or more children. Within the units were compounds comprised of four houses surrounded by a fence and having a common kitchen. A group of fifty boys lived together in a house that they themselves built.

In Panyido there's a river that doesn't dry up, with running water all year round. We were terribly hungry and wanted to catch some fish to fill our hollow stomachs. But how could we catch fish with no hooks or nets? We formed a spear by cutting a long, thin branch from a tree, shaving it, and hardening the wood in the fire. With that we caught a lot of fish.

Local people who lived in huts along the stream gave us problems when we first came to Panyido. 'Please, please can you just give us some corn?' we begged. 'We're hungry.'

But they killed us sometimes.

We received a lot of support from outside sources. American and European UN workers came to Panyido. Ethiopians brought tools for digging and for cutting the grass for our houses. Some Sudanese were a bit educated and worked with the Ethiopians.

Rada Banan, an NGO supported by the United Nations, adminis-
tered the schools and later even followed us to Kenya. Other
organizations provided food and medical care. But compared to
the number of boys, there was not much healthcare. If you had
diarrhea they'd say, 'Here, have an aspirin.'

Malaria was attacking me all the time. In 1989 I had a disease
with spots. It gives you a fever and diarrhea and I was really sick.
I had no medicine but thankfully after one week it disappeared
on its own.

Hygiene was a big problem. We had almost no clothes, maybe
one or two shirts each. We bathed in the river. Sometimes the
United Nations brought soap, but it would be gone after a week
and the rest of the month we had nothing. We used the same soap
for bathing, for washing clothes, and for cleaning pots. Most of
the time we just washed with water and nothing was very clean.
I think that's why many were catching diarrhea and dysentery and
were dying.

I started learning the ABCs when I went to school in Panyido.
There were no trained teachers, only friends from Sudan. Some had
gone to junior high or high school before the fighting began. The
disabled were the ones who taught us because they weren't able to
fight any more. The United Nations was the only group who took
responsibility for us—not the SPLA and not the Ethiopians.

Some of us had gone to school in Sudan before the war started.
At home in Bor I had begun grade one. Our northern government
had forced us to study in Arabic, but so much time had passed that
I couldn't remember anything. Now we were learning in English
with books that the United Nations provided, though we didn't
have enough. I studied from grade one up to grade four in Ethiopia
until we were forced to run away from there also.

We boys were all together, some older by two, three or four
years. We were almost all at the same level so they didn't divide
us by age.

'First you must build your classrooms,' we were told. 'And
then you can begin learning.'

We cut poles and grass and formed soil into mounds, starting low in the front row and higher in the back rows. The dirt mounds were our benches. We set up big logs around the edge and placed branches on top for a roof using tree fibers for ropes. A covering of grass kept the rain from penetrating, and mats were our walls.

One class had seventy or eighty children squeezed together. Some sat outside because there wasn't enough room inside.

We went to school five days a week, Monday through Friday. Sunday we went to church and Saturday was a wash day, when we went to the river and washed our clothes. During the week, after school we worked to cut grass.

Cartons of cooking oil were especially valuable if no oil had spilled on them. The tins of cooking oil came in cartons with US AID written on them. If they were clean it was a great opportunity to use them like an exercise book. Then if you had a pencil you could write on the cartons. Even the pencils we cut in pieces so everyone would have one.

Gabriel laughed as he remembered the primitive conditions at his school in Panyido.

We used to fight over the cartons. When they came into the camp you might tell the leader, 'That good one is mine.' But then someone else got it and you'd start quarreling. We were just a bunch of kids together. You could see boys clashing all the time.

I very much liked going to school. We were ready to learn even with so few materials and teachers.

We organized ourselves and the teachers would choose leaders—a leader of one thousand, of two hundred, of fifty and of ten. It was well organized actually. The teachers gave orders to the leader of the thousand and then on down.

They would tell us the plan for the day. 'Today some children will go to the forest to hew poles. Others will cut grass.'

If one was chosen to be the leader he tried to prove himself and bullied the others. Some of the boys were good leaders, but not all. A wise teacher might demote a leader who mistreated his fellows. It was really terrible not to have adults—just boys leading other boys.

It's difficult for children without parents. It's hard for one child to tell another what to do. You could tell them, 'Tomorrow you're on duty.' But you couldn't always enforce the rules. Some children didn't want to bathe. They were so grimy and smelly, but nothing could be done about it except to beat them.

Gabriel's description of Panyido, a camp of thousands of boys living with little adult supervision, both fascinated and horrified me. I thought about my children when they were young and so dependent on me.

Gabriel and his friends provided for all their own physical necessities in the harshest of conditions. They built their own homes and classrooms, as well as cooked meals and washed their clothes. Beyond that, they created surrogate families, attempting to somehow meet one another's emotional needs.

I am reminded of *Lord of the Flies*, a novel about a group of English school boys who landed on a deserted island and the type of society they formed. Their disastrous effort to govern themselves is meant as an allegory about human nature and culture. Many other books and movies have been produced on this theme.

When you first meet Gabriel today you wouldn't guess he suffered such physical and emotional deprivation in his childhood, especially when you hear his frequent, warm laughter. But as you spend more time with him, you become aware of an underlying sadness.

In many Sudanese we notice a fatalistic approach to life. They seem to accept any circumstances that come their way.

"Why don't they try to improve or change the situations they find themselves in?" John asked me. "They often seem unable to mobilize for improvement."

"Could this be a result of the traumas they've suffered?"

During the rainy season we studied. During the dry season school closed so we could rebuild our huts and classrooms. The rain was always against us. We had to make sure our living area didn't leak when the rains came. While going to school, we didn't do much work, only studying, cleaning and cooking.

With no grinding mills, we had to pound the maize to prepare it. That's a really terrible job and takes so much time. We first cut a big tree—one we thought was very strong—to be a mortar for pounding. We hollowed out a hole inside and smoothed it properly. Another big tree we made into the pestle. Afterwards we put it in water for a week, and then let it dry. Then we could start pounding the maize.

This tough task required lots of energy, so we took turns. We had to pound fifteen kilos (about 33 lbs) of maize into flour and sift it also. The maize is very hard. We pounded it to remove the outer shell and then soaked it in water the whole night to soften it. Early in the morning we took it from the water and put it on sacks to dry a bit so that when we put them in the mortar, the pounding was a bit easier. We made it into ugali, a sort of porridge.

Our group of two hundred had one pot—an oil drum cut in half. Our stove was three stones. We made a fire and placed the pot filled with water on the stones. Beans from the United Nations were the main ingredient, but sometimes there were no beans. So we went out to the bush and gathered plants we recognized from home to eat with our ugali. We had no meat. Later on we began our own gardens.

It was really difficult trying to do everything ourselves. We were too young and inexperienced to do everything the right way. The fire needs lots of wood. Beans need lots of cooking. Sometimes the beans weren't fully cooked and children became sick with diarrhea.

Panyido was a huge camp and we were just a bunch of boys desperate to survive. We felt we had no one helping us. We didn't even know the whereabouts of John Garang, our rebel leader whom we all considered to be our father. He was fighting for our freedom in south Sudan and had no time to see us, but his message reached us: 'Many of you will die, but those who remain will return to our homes later on.'

At this point Gabriel broke down in uncontrollable sobs. I didn't know how to react. I reached back and gently turned off the tape recorder.

What am I doing to this dear friend, causing him to cry? I wondered. Is it fair to ask him to relive these awful experiences? Or is it perhaps healing and therapeutic for him, better than bottling things up inside?

Gradually Gabriel composed himself and continued speaking.

Since 1983 we've been suffering. So I'm crying. But God knows our suffering. Although John Garang couldn't come to us in person to relieve our suffering, he was fighting for us, and his message reached us.

Bullets Like Rain

To understand this new people group who had landed on our doorstep, I felt I needed to learn some of Sudan's history.

As Gabriel told his story, certain dates seemed to be pivotal.

Britain's colonial rulers had encouraged a division between the Muslim north and the Christian or animist south, even forbidding contact between the two sides. As British rule began to weaken worldwide in the 1940s, they made plans to pull out of Sudan. With a population divided among about six hundred tribes who spoke over a hundred languages, Sudan was far from unified. The leading ethnic group was the Arab Muslim population, but the Dinka tribe represented the largest of the minorities.

In 1956 Sudan became the largest country in Africa as they gained their independence. This unfortunately only increased the tension between the north and the south. With Khartoum in the north serving as the capital of the new country and all power centered there, the southerners felt like second-class citizens. The Dinkas and other southern tribes began a rebellion and the country soon found itself in an all-out civil war.

In 1969 Jaafar Muhammad Numeiry led a military junta against Sudan's central government. In the beginning the southerners viewed him positively because he offered them the possibility of self-rule in the framework of a unified government. He abolished parliament however, and outlawed all political parties.

Finally in 1972 the Addis Abba agreement was signed and the south received its long hoped-for autonomy together with freedom of religion. Eleven years of peace began which lasted until 1983.

Further complicating the scenario, in 1978 an American company discovered oil in an area just south of the border between north and south Sudan. According to the Addis Abba Treaty, the south was accorded all profits from minerals or other deposits on their land. Numeiry, however, had no intention of surrendering the valuable oil fields. Oil became an important factor in the strife and remains so today.

The year 1983 kept repeating itself in the stories I was hearing from Gabriel and other Sudanese friends. Not only had the south's autonomy been gradually reduced, but in 1983 Numeiry exchanged his military uniform for a djellaba and declared sharia, the strict Muslim law code, throughout all Sudan. At the same time, the government initiated the policy of rotating army units between the north and south, which so angered the southern soldiers as Gabriel had explained to me.

A full-scale war broke out in 1983 between the Sudanese army of the north and the SPLA, the southern militia led by John Garang.

Now, as we drove toward Jerusalem, John and I listened as Gabriel continued his backseat narration into the recorder.

With the downfall of Mengistu Haile Mariam, the Marxist dictator of Ethiopia, in 1991 our region was thrown into great confusion. The United Nations, who had been helping us, fled.

The new government that overthrew Mengistu began fighting the southern Sudanese rebels. So we had to run from the camp in Panyido back to our home area that was now controlled by Arabs. This led to a suffering I will never forget.

Mengistu had been fighting a civil war against his own Ethiopian rebels who were based in northern Sudan, our enemy. He had welcomed Garang to Ethiopia, and had invited him to have bases there. But when those Ethiopian rebels took power, we had to leave. Together with the SPLA soldiers, we minors were forced to run back to south Sudan in the midst of serious battle.

The Ethiopians were against us because they were allied with the Sudanese army. We knew that they would either kill us or make us fight against the SPLA, our own people. Capturing us would be a big blow to the SPLA who used to call us their 'children.'

We had no choice but to leave the camp in Panyido that we'd built and lived in for three years and to head for the River Gilo.

Oh, I know that river well.

Gabriel sighed as he made this last statement. From the books I had read about the Lost Boys, a genre I had recently discovered, I knew that the Gilo River crossing was a terrible chapter in their lives. Until this trip to Jerusalem with Gabriel in our car, I hadn't connected him with the horrifying stories I had been reading. Now I understood that Gabriel's journey paralleled those in the books—thousands of boys as young as five or six fleeing on foot from Sudan to Ethiopia to Kenya and on the way braving wild animals, armed rebels, hunger and thirst.

The Ethiopian army was after us, trying to seize us. While their goal was to defeat the SPLA rebels, they also killed a lot of my friends.

When we reached the River Gilo, boys poured into the surging water while the soldiers shot at us. Most boys didn't grow up near a river so they couldn't swim and the rapid waters pulled them under. Friends next to me splashed, floundered and drowned. Hippos and crocodiles seized many of the children, dragged them under, and bit off legs or arms. I thank God because, though I was young, I was born next to a river and knew how to swim. As I swam across, I was protected by God till I reached the other side.

From there I trekked, with the thousands of children who survived, to Pochala in eastern Sudan on the Ethiopian border. In Pochala life was no better. The hunger and suffering was too much and many people died. We often heard about children who went outside of town to gather wood but were killed by gunmen. But even then the government continued bombing us with Antonovs.

'Don't target the civilians, the children and the women,' Christian aid organizations warned the Sudanese government.

I think they tried their best, but all they could do was to try to influence their own governments. The Sudanese government ignored them. From people who knew English and listened to the radio we heard that the U.S. government and the United Nations were condemning the government of Sudan for bombing children.

We depended, unfortunately, on our government to give permission for food drops. When the UN was finally allowed in, we had a bit of peace and relief from our hunger, except for our fights because we were too many people for too little food.

Besides the food drops I thanked God that there were a lot of trees, wild greens and vegetables. Our Almighty Father fed us through His nature. Later, an airfield was built and some planes landed with supplies.

During our three months in Pochala we were constantly being attacked by southern Sudanese tribes whom the Arabs supported. They were fighting against our protectors but also wanted to kill us children. Other tribes from the south were dividing us by saying that liberation will only be for the Dinka.

Those killing us were of the Anyuak tribe. They weren't happy to have us in their area. The Arabs confused them by claiming that we wanted to destroy them and grab their land and the Anyuak believed the Arab propaganda.

Liberation doesn't come easy. We were fighting for the good of us all and wanted some provisions. Some tribes will never understand that and think you're just looting them. They don't understand that it's for their benefit too.

The constant attacks from the militias made our stay in Pochala unbearable. So when we received a warning that the government troops were going to capture Pochala, the Red Cross together with our elders decided to let the 'minors,' as we were called, start walking.

I didn't go with the rest of the minors, but remained behind. I was living in Pochala with one of my father's wives and her children. The way was too long for my stepmother and her young children to walk. So I wasn't considered an unaccompanied minor.

One thing I'll never forget as long as I live is the attack on Pochala. It was on a Sunday. I went to church in the morning and never could have imagined what would happen after. Having nothing to do after church, I went with some of my friends to swim in the small river nearby.

At about 1:00 P.M. the government forces of Sudan surprised us with a sudden attack on the SPLA camp close to us, just on the other side of the river. The camp was nearly empty because most of the rebel soldiers had gone to town to see their relatives.

The government soldiers began shooting randomly. 'Run!' I yelled to my friends. 'Let's get out of here! Back to Pochala!'

I had no time to even put my clothes on. I had just been swimming in my underwear so I held my shirt and shorts in my hand. As I ran the bullets were whizzing by.

I remember one man running along behind me. Just as he passed me, a bullet hit him in the back and he fell. I nearly stepped on him.

Bullets were falling like drops of rain from rifles and from big artillery. I came to something like a valley with a big tree in the middle. A paralyzing fear overcame me when I saw people around me being hit. So I decided to take cover behind the tree. Bullets were even bouncing off the tree.

The minors had left Pochala in December, a month before the

area was attacked in January of 1992. If they hadn't left when they did, most of them probably would have died.

After forty minutes of gunfire, which seemed like hours, the rebels managed to repel the government troops. But all the displaced people were scattered.

When the roar of the guns died down, I came back to our hut and found that my stepmother and her children had disappeared. In the chaos, they had gone back to Bor but hadn't been able to take anything with them.

I was alone again.

When we didn't hear any more bullets we were sure the SPLA had defeated the enemy and hoped that those who ran away would come back. But as the SPLA were rejoicing in their victory, the enemy was deploying troops with more artillery. They had a lot more weapons than the SPLA did.

Three hours later the enemy returned and that's when the big rockets started shelling and bombarding our houses—mere huts, thatched with grass. As bombs struck, the houses burst into fire. A powerful, driving hot wind flamed the blaze.

We heard the booming sound of the artillery from the government forces assaulting the SPLA positions. But the SPLA couldn't withstand them. Some of our soldiers started running away from their stations.

The wind was violent. I didn't know what to do. I didn't even have shoes, and we were running in thorn bushes. If you were lucky, you had a pair of sandals made from tires. I had some but they were put together with nails, which fell out as I ran and the sandals became useless.

As it was getting dark, I came upon a big SPLA truck trying to pick up the wounded, but the driver had only two people to help carry the many injured. By this time the area was almost completely in the control of the government forces.

I heard the truck driver saying, 'Please bring the wounded over here, so we can go!'

But no one helped because we were afraid. We would have had to move in the direction of the enemy to pick up those injured, and the enemy was so close I could hear their voices.

When I jumped in the truck I found only five wounded adults. I immediately noticed that one of them was my cousin. He had blood squirting from his leg. His leg was shot completely through the bone. Later his leg was cut off. I think he's in Kenya now.

The problem was, the vehicle had no brakes, so we had to use a big stone to stop the tires from rolling. It also had no starter, so we had to station it on a hill where you could roll it. And there were only three of us to push it. But that's how we escaped.

We drove under fire from the enemy's bullets, but thank God they missed us. As we found other injured people on the way we stopped and put them inside until we crossed the river.

We were going through a small desert toward Boma, one of the towns in Jonglei state that was controlled by the SPLA. It was a two day drive, but we didn't have enough fuel. In the middle of the desert we met the head of the Red Cross for that area.

'Please,' our driver begged. 'Call the Red Cross on your radio to come take our wounded and these minors to Kenya.'

When we reached Boma I met some of my young friends. It had taken them two weeks to walk there. We used a shortcut through the desert because we were in a vehicle. If they had gone that way, they would have died of thirst.

I continued on with the Lost Boys. Our numbers were still in the thousands. The Red Cross was helping us. Having no other transportation for this large number of minors, we walked through the desert to Kenya, a distance of more than one thousand kilometers (more than six hundred twenty miles). Adding to that difficulty, we had to watch out for hostile tribes and government-controlled areas. They could intercept and ambush us on the way.

Because the 'road' was nearly non-existent, we could only use vehicles that could travel off-road. The only solution was to bring in water tankers. Those who couldn't walk could ride in the trucks.

The southern rebel forces were divided. Dr. Riek Machar, one of the SPLA leaders from the Nuer tribe, revolted against John Garang. He had a huge army that John Garang had originally armed.

I'll never forget the destruction in which many from my hometown of Bor were killed. The Arabs engineered the slaughter using all available means. They knew that Garang was too tough to defeat, so their goal was to infiltrate the SPLA and to usurp the leadership. They thought to use Dr. Machar because, with a doctorate in engineering he was highly respected. Garang and Machar both had doctorates, but Garang had more experience in the army. The Arabs believed that if Machar's forces destroyed Bor, the home of John Garang, the war would stop and they would have the victory.

So when Machar and his Nuer people came in 1991, he invaded Bor with a huge army and completely wiped out the area. They turned against us and killed everyone, including women and children. The destruction and genocide in Bor was shocking.

My mother, who had been living in Bor, ran away at that time and was hiding in the bush. My father, whom I hadn't heard from since 1983, ran in a different direction. He was captured by the government—tortured and killed, I heard later. Others told me that he died of natural causes. No one could accurately explain his death to me. A lot of my relatives were killed.

Machar and Garang reconciled before Garang died. I thank God because though what happened in 1991 was not good, we are Christians and we forgive each other.

In 2005, with the signing of the peace agreement between the Sudanese government and the SPLA, John Garang was sworn in as vice president, the second most powerful person in the country. He was the first Christian or southerner to hold such a high government post, which gave many Sudanese as well as observers renewed hope for Sudan's future. Three weeks later the helicopter in which he was returning from a meeting in Uganda crashed due to poor weather, it was said. Doubts exist, however, concerning the true reason for the accident.

Who Can See Me?

Sudan's war has been called the world's longest and most destructive civil conflict[1], horrifying even by the usual standards of war or in comparison with other disasters in Africa. According to the Women's Refugee Commission, two million people are estimated to have died in Sudan since 1983, and eighty percent of the population of five million people has been displaced at one time or another since that year[2]. Perhaps the only way to partially grasp the catastrophe is to meet people like Gabriel and to clothe the statistics with human faces. Then multiply millions of times.

Jafaar Numieri, who became infamous for introducing punishments such as public amputations, stoning, crucifixion and flogging, was ousted in a military coup in 1985. Civilian rule floundered for a few years until Colonel Omar Hassan al-Bashir and his Islamic Front seized power in another military coup in 1989.

The infighting in the SPLA between the two factions helped the government in its propaganda campaign to convince the world that the atrocities in southern Sudan were simply an internal conflict among tribes. They attempted to explain the unprecedented violence as tribal warfare between the Dinkas, led by John Garang, and the Nuer tribe under Riek Machar's leadership.

Even after reading books about the "Lost Boys," many aspects of Sudanese history are difficult to understand. Yet, although the schism between Garang and Machar was a low point in their battle for independence, it seems clear to me that the conflict in south Sudan was a premeditated campaign by north Sudan against the south.

I could write a book about our journey from Pochala to Kenya. We were pushed to our limits, physically and mentally. Our enemies ambushed and killed children on the way. We received miniscule amounts of water distributed in tiny cups.

But eventually we managed to reach the area of Kapoeta, a city in Sudan's Eastern Equatoria state. Thousands of us settled in a

---

1. http://www.iht.com/articles/2003/10/28/ederic_ed3_.php
2. http://www.womenscommission.org/fromthefield/sudan/110906.php

camp in nearby Narus. Although the Red Cross was helping, our life there was so difficult. We didn't know how long we'd stay so we started building schools like in Panyido. Kenya wasn't very far away, only about fifty kilometers to the border.

We had been in Narus for nearly two months when in May 1992, Kapoeta was assaulted and captured by the government. We knew that since Kapoeta was close to Narus we would be the next target.

'Time to move!' our elders told us around 6 P.M. 'Be ready to leave in an hour! We're not safe here any more.'

We began walking and didn't stop the whole night. Those who were strong arrived in Lokichokio, on the Kenyan Sudanese border, early in the morning. The rest trekked through the next day and by 4:00 P.M. everyone was there.

Two weeks later, the word came again, 'You're moving on! We're taking you to Kakuma, a town in northern Kenya.'

This time they transported us in trucks.

Kakuma was a complete wasteland. The area is semi-desert with no decent trees for making shelters. With the strong winds and scorching temperatures, we felt we were living in an oven. The United Nations began providing poles, plastic sheets and branches to make shelters, and food also.

A lot of us died in the camp from malnutrition. After many days of not eating, if you receive nutritious food like beans or flour, you'll eat anything to satisfy yourself but your body can't absorb it. So many boys suffered from diarrhea, dysentery and even cholera. But there wasn't proper sanitation, not even toilets. With no doctors, many children lost their lives when we came to Kakuma.

Another big problem at that camp was the Turkana, the local people. Those people were fighting us there and started killing us. Our life was so bad.

I hated especially the way the Kenyan police treated us during the rule of Daniel arap Moi, Kenya's president. When the police came into the camp they would enter our houses and help themselves to anything we had brought from Sudan. They would steal your radio, if you had one.

'Bring the receipt! Where's your receipt for the radio?' they would demand.

They knew we ran away from Sudan. We might have received that radio from someone fighting in the war. So how could we produce a receipt? Instead of welcoming us as friends or as neighbors, they treated us worse than the Arabs had.

They said, 'We're not the ones who caused the problem. We didn't invite you here. It's your leaders, John Garang and al-Bashir.'

They even took the food rations we received from the UN. If you refused, they killed you.

I couldn't bear that life anymore so I decided to return to Sudan. I traveled with some friends, among the thousands who returned from Kakuma to southern Sudan. We wanted to go back because our present life was unbearable. We thought it would be better to live a dignified life in Sudan than to be subject to all the suffering, temptations and humiliations we faced in Kenya.

Most of us had never experienced a situation as in Kenya. In Ethiopia, although we had nothing, we lived quietly and were worshipping God. But when the Kenyan police wanted to loot our goods, we felt frustrated and defenseless and reasoned it would be better to go back home.

The Kenyan police harassed us on the way. At each roadblock between Kakuma and Lokichokio we were taken out of the pickup and the police demanded money.

'Show us your passport!' they demanded.

'We're from the south,' we answered. 'In 1987 we ran away from our village to Ethiopia. Now we're going back.'

Who could have given us a passport? Where could we get money? We only received rations. If you stopped eating, you could sell your rations. After saving for some months, then maybe you could buy a ticket to travel.

Unfortunately many children became criminals. Although we had been oppressed for so long, we tried to control ourselves because from our church background we knew stealing was wrong. We also remembered stories from our youth. In the village everyone heard about you if you did something wrong.

In those days some people even committed suicide rather than have a bad name.

Gabriel's words caused me to reflect on a phenomenon we were observing among the Sudanese in Eilat. As we came to know them better and became involved in their lives, we were disappointed by instances of immorality. Moriah and Tom, our daughter and son-in-law, lived in an apartment next to the Sudanese housing on the kibbutz. They told us about police being called in the middle of the night to deal with skirmishes among the refugees. The cause was usually jealousy and sexual sin. A woman whom we knew very well and considered to have one of the more stable marriages was found in bed with a single man.

'Could it have to do with the fact that they are refugees and their society has been ripped apart?' I asked John.

With strong social taboos, their village life didn't allow people to get away with such behavior. People knew what their neighbors were doing and the whole village educated the children.

Gabriel and others were distressed by the conduct of those who crossed the moral boundaries.

I felt like an animal stuck in a trap. In 1991 I was about fourteen years old, the age that boys were called up to fight. So if either the rebels or the government caught me, I'd be forced to become a soldier. With no one to help us and knowing that we weren't strong enough for combat, we boys were running from place to place.

Our big fear was that if the government captured us they would change our belief and train us in the Muslim religion and to become fighters. The problem with the rebels was that, although they officially only took boys who were seventeen or eighteen years old, they didn't know your actual age.

I became a Christian in 1987 and was baptized in Ethiopia. I knew about God already from my home, but wasn't yet baptized.

In Ethiopia we had churches, priests, pastors and evangelists;

but they were being killed by the Arabs. If you spoke about God and Jesus Christ in an area controlled by the government you could be sure you wouldn't live another day.

In the SPLA-held areas, however, everyone was free to believe as he liked, because the rebels were fighting for freedom for everyone—Christians, Muslims, and believers in traditional African religions.

I remember Paulo Deng Chol, a Christian evangelist from Bor. A Dinka and a man of exceptionally strong faith, he preached with such power that you could never forget his messages.

Another man who influenced my life was Pastor Andrew Mayol Majak. I met him in Panyido. I don't know whether he's alive or has been killed because he was also evangelizing in south Sudan where anything could have happened to him. We Sudanese are experts at keeping in touch and have strong networks to locate people; but it's impossible to find everyone.

Pastor Andrew used to encourage us in the Bible, which was actually our main sustenance at that time when we had little else. Most of the boys who managed to survive were those who held on to God and the Bible. Pastor Andrew read the gospels to us and drew examples from the Old Testament.

'After the children of Israel fled Egypt, they wandered in the wilderness for forty years and suffered tremendous hardships. Enemies attacked them and they lacked food and water,' he explained to us. 'But God promised them they would later find safety if they remained obedient to Him. If they rebelled, there would be trouble. Therefore we also, though desperately poor in the world's goods, should aim to be rich in God's Spirit.'

So, though we had nothing—no clothes or food—our faith was very strong. Death, disease and hunger surrounded us, but the Word of God gave us strength to wait patiently for the time of plenty. We trusted God and praised Him through all our tribulations.

Any difficulties I experience today cannot even be called 'problems' compared to what we went through in those days. We have no hunger or diseases here. And since 1987 I've been a believer in Jesus Christ.

So I went back from Kenya to Sudan. I ran from place to place and hid myself. By this time I had a bit of education. In Kenya I nearly completed grade six. A fine Italian Catholic priest called Father Vincent established a technical school and invited me to join. I enjoyed learning the basics of masonry—bricklaying, plastering and flooring. It wasn't advanced and I didn't manage to complete the year's course, but afterwards I could do basic construction.

I was hoping to find an organization that would help me in south Sudan. I planned to tell them, 'If you protect me, I will help you, even if you can only give me a hut to live in.'

I went to a place called New Cush in Eastern Sudan (Sudan and Ethiopia used to be called Cush.) I was working in construction with a Sudanese NGO called SRRA, The Sudan Relief and Rehabilitation Association. But the area was attacked constantly.

I hoped to find my family and to reconnect with them after over ten years of separation. That was my main goal in returning to Sudan. I never managed to find my parents, though. When I tried to trace my sisters, the only news I received was that one of their husbands had been killed.

I stayed there in New Cush from April 1995 until December 1996. I feared being forced to join our army and fight, or of being caught by the Arabs.

Finally I prayed, 'Lord, what shall I do?'

I knew I wasn't eligible to receive UN refugee status in Kenya a second time and without it I would suffer a lot. On the other hand, I would never receive permission to leave Sudan. The leader of the NGO I worked for was a former SPLA commander. He ran the organization as a military man. Everything had to do with work and output, although we were given no wages, just food sometimes. Since there was no way to reason with him, I just ran away.

I walked the whole night through the mountains of the Eastern Equatoria to a place called Natinga which means 'Who can see me?' in Dinka. After John Garang fled with his followers from populated areas to the edge of Sudan, he founded Natinga as a hiding place and gave it that name.

The NGO I worked for had no money, so my salary for

a month of backbreaking work was a carton of oil with 'USA' written on it. By selling the oil and my rations, I had some money for my trip.

"Ready for a break?" John asked. "We're at the Dead Sea. We've been traveling two and a half hours and have another hour and a half till Jerusalem. We'll stop here, have something to eat, use the bathroom, and float in the Dead Sea."

As we stepped out of the car into the blistering dry air, I wondered how Gabriel was feeling. Just listening to him methodically narrate his life history had my head spinning. It seemed to me that the words "very hard," "so difficult" and "suffering" kept repeating themselves.

Yet, except for the time when he burst into tears, Gabriel appeared to emotionally divorce himself from the extreme hardships he'd experienced. I had difficulty connecting this calm, intelligent, handsome man with that malnourished, half-naked young boy running from place to place.

"Let's first have lunch," John said. "Gabriel, what would you like? Maybe a sandwich and a drink?"

"No, that's okay," answered Gabriel. "I'm fine."

What? I thought. *Not hungry?* It was lunch time and he probably didn't have time to eat breakfast before we left.

"Come on," I insisted. "We'll all have cheese sandwiches."

Suddenly I felt it was absolutely necessary to provide Gabriel with food as if to make up for all those years of hunger—starvation, actually. I reasoned that Gabriel's whole concept of meals must be different from ours.

And what about our need to help Gabriel? Was this common among aid workers—an overwhelming desire to offer support? I could imagine this becoming a problem. Buying lunch for Gabriel wasn't a big deal, but we would need a lot of wisdom in the long run to understand how to truly be of assistance. Even within our family we had different approaches.

We had already run into issues with our Sudanese boys. John had the habit of being very lenient with them.

"I like buying them things and taking them places," he would say. "They're from Sudan. They've never had anything and now I can help them."

"But Abba," our children responded. "You didn't spoil us, so why spoil these boys? You have to discipline them more."

"I'm like their grandfather," John insisted. "Grandparents aren't the ones to discipline. I'm showing them love and acceptance. That's what they need, and a safe home where they're always welcome."

We have to find the balance, I thought.

The Fugitive

"Can you remember where you left off?" I asked Gabriel as we sat in the car again and continued our trip to Jerusalem.

"Sure," he said. "I was in Natinga, on the way back to Kenya."

"I'm amazed how well you remember the fine points and dates of all your journeys. Have you ever told anyone your story before?"

"I told it a few times in Cairo, but never in such detail because it's really too long and too sad. But those are things I could never forget."

"How did you like swimming in the Dead Sea?" asked John. "Or should I say floating?"

"It's amazing. I'm glad we stopped," Gabriel said.

I had money from selling the oil. With those funds to sustain me, I walked a long distance in the night through the Toposa's territory. They're well-armed and they just roam the area killing people and are the same people who were attacking us in Kapoeta. The Almighty God protected me until I found a ride to Lokichokio.

I can tell you firmly I endured a lot in my life, but the suffering has taught me many lessons. I learned to be humble, to appreciate the simple life, and to be satisfied with whatever I have.

On January 1, 1997 I came back to Lokichokio. I wondered what I should do. Go back to Kakuma? It would be a long process for me to be re-accepted.

I went to the police immigration on the border in Lokichokio and said to them, 'I'm not feeling well and need to go to Nairobi. Can you give me a one month travel permit? I'll pay you money.' So I bribed them and they gave me three months of travel time.

It's a long distance from Lokichokio to Nairobi, the capital of Kenya, over one thousand kilometers. Since I didn't have anything to eat along the way, I bought sweets and some mandazi, a deep-fried bread that Kenyans eat, sort of like a doughnut.

When I reached Nairobi I tried to contact the UN office. I still had $150 in my pocket left after paying $150 in bribes. I stayed in one of the large slums in Nairobi. The filth, overcrowding, constant racket, foul smells, crime, drugs and open sewers made life impossible. I was searching for a decent and peaceful place to live, but this certainly wasn't it.

"Judy and I were in Nairobi in 2004," John said. "Some Kenyan friends took us into one of the slums to go shopping. We met some Sudanese there. Wow, that slum was a whole city in itself. So many people crammed into a small area and tons of kids."

I decided to keep moving. I prayed for someone to give me money so I could go to Tanzania and just die there if it was God's will. That was my wish because life was so painful. I didn't know what to do but I heard that Father Vincent, the Catholic priest, had left Kakuma for Nairobi, so I was trying to trace him. I hoped he could assist me somehow. He belonged to the Salesian Society that was founded by Father John Bosco.

John added, "Hey, I was in the Bosco School in my town in Holland. I was brought up as a Catholic." John had found something in common, a point of contact, with Gabriel.

I never found Father Vincent but I did reach the Salesians. They helped me with a little food and money and a few papers, but it wasn't enough. So I began asking some Sudanese who had money. Each one gave me a little until I reached about $300 again.

If you have money, you can do anything. My aim was to take a bus from Nairobi to Dar es Salaam, the biggest city in Tanzania. I'd heard of a large refugee camp there for Burundians and Rwandans, so I thought to ask the UN if I could join them.

It was on January 15th of 1997, at 7:00 P.M., that I boarded a bus heading to Tanzania. All the passengers were Kenyans and Tanzanians except for me. When we stopped on the border, before reaching the town of Arusha, my worst fear was realized—I would be caught. Each person traveling on the bus had to get off. The immigration workers were checking us, and everyone else showed their passports, but of course I didn't have one. So I ran away and hid myself. But the problem was that I had left a small bag on the bus and had no way of retrieving it. The bags were taken into the customs house and checked by the authorities.

One man asked, 'Who owns this bag?'

I noticed another official monitoring my movements and realized I was in trouble. So I came out of hiding and lined up with those whose bags and passports were being examined. After they checked my bag I hid again. And I praise my Lord they didn't see me.

There still was another danger. After checking, they would mark something on the bag. All the bags that were checked had that sign, but mine didn't. The long, tedious process took hours. Around 3:00 A.M. we were supposed to leave for Dar es Salaam.

While I was trying to remain in the shadows, a drunken man approached me. I could tell he wanted something from me, and I knew I should go along with him or else he'd report me.

'Man, I know you,' he mumbled. 'You're Sudanese and don't have a passport. If you don't want to suffer, you must give me something.'

I lied and told him, 'My friend, I'm on my way to Arusha where my brother works. The immigration workers were checking us. If you wait for me here tomorrow I'll come with money and give you $100.'

I didn't tell him the truth or else he would have notified the police and the immigration workers.

Gabriel laughed about fooling the drunkard. He sounded as if he was telling a story that happened just a few days ago.

Because he was drunk he believed me. So he didn't tell the officials that I was the owner of the bag and they left me alone. I was lucky.

Early in the morning there were two identical buses. I was still in hiding. When I saw one of the buses pulling out I stood in the middle of the road because I thought it was my bus. If it went without me, what would become of my life?

So I stood in the middle of the road and didn't care what anyone thought about me. I could imagine them saying, 'Why's that crazy guy standing in the middle of the road?'

Gabriel laughed again. I loved it when he laughed. Most of the time he seemed a little too serious.

It's healthy for him, I thought, *to be able now to see the humor in situations which were at the time a question of life and death.*

The bus driver halted and I quickly jumped in. I told him, 'I'm going with you.'

But I soon realized I didn't recognize any of the passengers and started yelling. 'Please, let me off! This isn't my bus!'

The bus driver, a good man, turned around and drove back to the station for me so I could wait for the correct bus.

When my fellow passengers in my bus saw me, they all laughed and were happy. 'How did you manage?' they asked.

'I managed by the help of God,' I answered and stepped inside.

Before we left Nairobi the bus driver said to me, 'My friend, since you don't have a passport, I don't know how I can help you.'

'Don't worry,' I told him. 'God will help me.'

'I don't know how He'll help,' he said. 'But try your luck and if you're caught it's your problem.'

I crossed the border into Tanzania without any more problems.

On the way to Dar es Salaam I met a man from Uganda. He worked for a construction company and was on a business trip. He was now on his way to Harare in Zimbabwe.

He told me, 'Here in Tanzania your life will be tough. Without speaking Swahili you'll have a difficult time getting around. I'd like to help you. I suggest you go to Zimbabwe. There are many Sudanese there, especially in Harare, and most of them are Dinka. John Garang has an office there because they have a relationship with President Robert Mugabe. The UN there will assist you and since you're young enough they'll send you to school.'

'Are you certain?' I asked.

'Surely,' he answered.

'But I don't have money to go through Zambia,' I told him. 'What can I do?'

'Don't worry. Just buy a ticket here,' he said.

So right there I changed my plans and we went together. Instead of staying in Tanzania, I decided to go on to Zimbabwe. I still had $100. I bought a ticket on TANZARA, which stands for Tanzanian Zambian Railroad.

He asked me to travel in first class with him. I chose third class, however, to be with my own people and also I knew that I needed to save money to use later.

'Won't they catch me on the way?' I asked, knowing we'd be on the train a long time with twenty stops.

'Don't worry,' he said. 'If your money is finished, I'll help you. Your people are good. I know they'll pay me back when you reach Harare.'

Again, as a refugee with no passport I felt terrible stress as I boarded the train from Dar es Salaam to Lusaka in Zambia, a three days' journey.

We Dinka are different from other Africans and easily recognized. Most of us are tall, dark and slim.

After I had bought the ticket, the migration police said to me, 'My friend, I know you're Sudanese. Hurry!' he told me. 'We just had some Sudanese here who came from Nairobi like you. We beat and deported them. So, my friend, talk like a man.'

To 'talk like a man' in the language of East Africa means to give a bribe.

Gabriel laughed. I didn't find the corruption particularly funny and I'm sure he didn't either, but I think he enjoyed introducing us to the craziness of life in Africa. Obviously, refugees were particularly vulnerable to the whims of officials and bureaucrats.

The policeman demanded, 'Friend, give me five hundred. If you fail to do that, you'll be thrown in prison and then deported back to Sudan.'

I began trembling. I knew I wouldn't be sent to south Sudan but directly to Khartoum because the Tanzanian and Sudanese governments have a relationship. In Tanzania, though there are many Christians, most of the population is Muslim, especially on the island of Zanzibar.

I feared that if I were sent back to Sudan or even to Nairobi, I would be tortured in prison and even killed.

'My friends, please help me,' I begged those police. 'You know that south Sudan is at war. We don't have passports. I tried to get refugee status in Kenya, but no one helped me. Please let me just pass through your country and go to Zimbabwe. I'm no harm to your land.'

'Sure. Just give me five hundred,' he insisted.

John interrupted and asked, "How much is five hundred shillings?"

"Not shillings," Gabriel answered. "Five hundred dollars! A ridiculous sum."

'*F*rankly, my friend,' I told that officer, 'I have only $100 in my pocket and this is my whole life—my food on the way and my transport to Zimbabwe.'

'No way!' he answered. 'What's $100? Are you joking?'

'I'm not joking. I'm in trouble. I don't have money,' I pleaded.

They put me in a small room and started pushing me around and checking me. I had hidden each $20 in different pockets. But they found it all and I was left with nothing.

'I could be caught again. I know that God takes care of me, but I need you to write a letter and stamp it so that no one will touch me on the way.'

Because they were corrupt people, they wouldn't do it.

'Then I'm not going,' I stubbornly told that policeman.

He finally wrote something down, pretending to stamp it. But he was deceiving me. Then he called me and said, 'Okay, go.'

One Day You Will Be Free

After our "Fun Day" on the beach with the Sudanese children in May, we all agreed we should keep up the momentum. We wanted to get to know them better, to provide more fun times for the children, and to assist the adults in any way necessary.

Only now, hearing Gabriel's story in detail was I beginning to develop a broader understanding of the trials facing refugees. Someone meeting Gabriel for the first time would see a tall, attractive, intelligent man, who speaks fluent English. They would have no clue as to the emotional and physical burdens he carries. And Gabriel was just one of the hundreds of Sudanese refugees who were showing up in our city. We had no illusions about helping the whole world, but surely we could make a difference in the lives of some of these needy people.

John and I felt it wasn't an option for us to ignore the refugees, a people whom God loves.

God entered my life when I came to Israel in 1973. Four years earlier I had left the comfortable suburb in which I grew up and sought to find answers to life's questions in a small Eskimo village above the Arctic Circle. I thought that by living a life close to nature and away from the entrapments of modern civilization, I would find the true meaning and purpose of life.

I grew to love the stark, wild Alaskan landscapes and the basic, primitive lifestyle. But after three years I felt restless again and decided to move on. Traveling and working my way slowly through Europe, my goal was to eventually join an ashram in India. I lived in a cave in Morocco, in a chateau in Switzerland, and on a beach in Crete. After one year on the road I was exhausted from the nomadic lifestyle and decided to stop in Israel before beginning the strenuous overland route to India. In Israel I could connect with my Jewish roots and meet distant relatives who would hopefully provide me with a warm bed and meals.

Israel fascinated me—a land where east meets west, modern meets ancient, Moses meets Jesus. I decided that to understand this land of contradictions and contrasts I needed to read the Bible.

Having already read many religious and spiritual books, I immediately realized the Bible was different. God Himself was speaking to mankind, to me. "Thus says the Lord," I read over and over. Prophecies were fulfilled. Even the state of Israel was proof. "I will build you up again and you will be rebuilt. ... I will ... gather them from the ends of the earth" (Jeremiah 31:4, 8).

But what about Jesus? In our tradition he was at worst a liar and deceiver and at best a misguided rabbi. Yet in reading the

New Testament, I discovered an extraordinary, loving man who had a way of connecting personally with everyone he met, even the outcasts of society. Jesus said of himself, "I am the way and the truth and the life. No one comes to the Father except through me" (John 14:6).

I was falling in love with Jesus and came to the point in my reading and thinking where I had no choice but to accept Him as my guide and the Bible as my guidebook. My life turned completely around, and I found an inner peace I'd never dreamed of. I wanted to act more like Jesus, with his compassion, patience and joy of life.

In my hippy lifestyle, I had been trying to relax and "go with the flow," but I wasn't succeeding. I discovered that Jesus could help me because He said, "Do not worry about tomorrow, for tomorrow will worry about its own things. Sufficient for the day is its own trouble" (Matthew 6:33).

After I married John, we moved to Eilat in 1976 and searched for people to love like Jesus loves. In the beginning the hippies and travelers were the strangers in our town. After the Iron Curtain fell in 1990 and the Russian Jews began immigrating by the hundreds of thousands to Israel, nearly all forty beds in our hostel were occupied by Russians including eighty-year-old babushkas (grandmothers).

After that, Romanian and Chinese construction workers came to Israel to build new neighborhoods and shopping malls. We found that they gratefully accepted invitations to the Shelter, responding positively to people who would treat them as fellow human beings.

So when the Sudanese began appearing on our streets, we knew we should help them as well. In the Gospel of Matthew when Jesus was speaking to His disciples about His return and His judgment, He said about the righteous, "I was hungry and you gave me something to eat, I was thirsty and you gave me something to drink, I was a stranger and you invited me in. I needed clothes and you clothed me, I was sick and you looked after me, I was in prison and you came to visit me ... Whatever you did for one of the least of these brothers of mine, you did for me" (Matthew 25:35, 40). Didn't this include the Sudanese refugees in Eilat?

We traveled on the train together, the Ugandan and I. He came to visit me in my third class car; I wasn't allowed to enter his first class section where they had beds and food. We poor people were crowded onto hard benches and the toilets were all stopped up.

'Gabriel, how are you?' he asked me.

'I'm fine,' I told him, though it was really a dreadful trip.

'Don't worry,' he tried to encourage me.

I went right through Tanzania and had no more problems. Three days after leaving Nairobi, on January 17, 1997 we reached Kabwe, Zambia. That's where immigration workers entered the train, checking for each person's passport.

Gabriel laughed as if thinking, 'Here we go again!'

They discovered me. But because they spoke English and I knew a bit of English also, the interaction was easier than on the Tanzanian border.

'No passport?' they questioned me. 'Where are you from?'

I introduced myself and found they knew a little about Sudan.

'Your country's problems are none of our business,' they said. 'This is a Christian nation and we abide by the law. If you don't have a passport you cannot enter.'

'Since this is supposed to be a Christian country, and I'm being persecuted by the Muslims, you should welcome me,' I said. 'At least allow me in Zambia if you don't allow me to go to Zimbabwe.'

'Forget about that,' he said. 'We just want to see your passport.'

I was desperate and tried to convince them. 'I told you,

I'm from a war-torn country and we don't have passports. I'm
searching for the UN to help me.'

'That's none of our business,' they insisted. They took me to
the police station. During the police interrogation one very good
man saw me and came running. 'I'll help you,' he said. 'Pray
to your God.'

He told the police, 'Please let me help this guy. I've heard a
lot of news from Sudan and they're suffering horribly, especially
in the south. Don't take him to prison. I'll care for him.'

But they refused.

'My brother, don't worry,' I told him. 'I have suffered up till
today. Only by God's grace I'm alive. I know He won't leave
me now. You're trying your best, but these officers don't want to
understand. So just let them do their job.'

I turned to the guard. 'I'll go with you. God will provide for
me.' I went with them into the jail.

'Do you have money?' they asked me.

I checked my pockets and found $10. I didn't know where it
came from. 'Here's $10, but there's no more.'

They shoved me into a small room of three square meters with
ten other people. When you needed to use the toilet everyone could
see you. That jail was so bad.

If you wanted to eat, you had to provide for yourself. You
could buy a piece of old, dry bread and a few grams of sugar.
Then mixing the sugar with water, you drank it with your bread
and those were our rations.

For the three days on the train I had only eaten biscuits and
water; but in that jail I didn't have an appetite because in my heart
I was worried. Even when that Ugandan guy came and wanted to
give me a piece of bread and some sugar water I couldn't eat.

'Sorry. A little water is all I can take now,' I told him 'Those
guys inside the jail are attacking me and trying to rob me. They're
trying to put their hands in my pockets.'

'My friend, where are you from?' one guy in my cell asked.

'I'm not a Zambian and I'm not a criminal. If the rest of you
are criminals here, you ought to respect me. Why do people treat

me like this?' I was annoyed. I gave him the bread, water and
sugar that my Ugandan friend had brought me, and he was happy
and became my friend.

'Why aren't you eating?' he asked. 'You look weak and
hungry.'

'I have a lot of problems, but don't worry,' I answered. 'I
have no appetite. Just eat.'

I spent the night there and early in the morning the police
came to question me.

'Where are you from?' they asked me.

'I'm from south Sudan.' I explained to them my troubles.

'Okay. We're taking you to the refugee camp.'

Gabriel laughed, but I didn't understand what was so funny. As
he continued his story, however, the ploy soon became clear.

After just twenty minutes, I found myself in Zambia's most
stringent maximum security prison.

"Not a refugee camp?" questioned John.

"Not a refugee camp," Gabriel answered.

"They were lying to you?" John asked.

"They were lying to me. And because the war in Sudan had
scattered us, I found other friends there who were Lost Boys
also. I couldn't believe they had been in prison for three months
already."

The jail was a terrible, terrible, terrible. We only had one
meager meal a day, at noon—mainly maize (corn), beans, and
watery soup. It was extremely cold at the time, colder than I'd ever
experienced in Sudan, and they didn't give us blankets. We were
locked inside from 3 P.M. till 9 A.M. so I spent six months without

seeing the moon. While there I suffered from malaria and diarrhea and they gave me no treatment.

But because of all my problems I turned to God. And I know it was my God who released me.

We weren't allowed visitors except for Father Bent, a priest who came to pray with us and knew a lot about Sudan. When Father Bent first came—what a wonderful man he was—he told us, 'I heard the news from south Sudan and that you are fighting the Arabs. I know the suffering of you Christians. Don't worry, my sons. Take God as your protector. I will go to the UN office. Why should you be kept in prison as if you were criminals when they know you come from a war zone?'

The officer in charge actually loved us and wanted to release us. He used to even eat with us. He sometimes called us to his office and said, 'My friends, I know you have caused no problems. I told the immigration people, "Why are you holding these poor Sudanese in prison? They aren't criminals. They ran away from war. They aren't making problems, so please release them."'

Congolese, Rwandan and Burundian refugees were also in prison with us. I remember one child whose arm was cut off. He stayed with his mother in the women's jail. Another woman from Burundi gave birth there. I couldn't understand. Why keep a woman in prison until she gives birth? Her husband was with their other child on the men's side.

So we were all together in that maximum security prison. Father Bent provided us with books, and we even started studying in prison.

'One day you will be free,' he encouraged us.

Back to School

Ketziot Prison sprawls over a large, flat, sunburned area near Israel's border with Egypt. Built as a prison for Palestinian security prisoners, it has a new wing for African refugees consisting of caravans surrounded by barbed wire.

Although desperate Africans from Ivory Coast, Liberia, Mauritania, Congo and other countries, had been streaming into Spain, Italy, Malta and the Canary Islands in makeshift, flimsy boats, they hadn't yet discovered Israel. However, in our era of media saturation and mobile phones in even the tiniest, most remote villages word spread quickly. The passage across the barren desert from Egypt to Israel became a "highway for those with nothing to lose" (*Jerusalem Post*, March 31, 2008).

For many refugees, Ketziot is their first address in Israel, but it's not exactly a comfortable home. Men and women live separately, and although prisoners receive three meals a day, they have nothing to do to combat the boredom.

The security issue has been an excuse to lock them up—Sudanese come from a country at enmity with Israel. Particularly the earlier arrivals, such as Gabriel in 2006, were sent automatically to prison. Meanwhile, human rights groups labored to have them released. And as Ketziot filled up with refugees, later arrivals were sent right from the border, after a thorough security check to make sure they weren't terrorists, to the streets of Beer Sheva or Tel Aviv.

Many of us have felt enraged at the conditions in Ketziot. But when I heard Gabriel speak about the maximum security prison in Zambia, Ketziot sounded like a country club. Yet they still were enclosed and their future was unclear. I wondered whether Gabriel when he was incarcerated in Ketziot, remembered the words of Father Bent: "One day you will be free."

Having no established refugee policy, Israel is divided between those who believe we have a moral duty to help refugees who arrive on our shores, particularly in light of the Holocaust suffered by the Jewish people, and those who believe we have enough problems of our own in Israel without getting involved in the suffering of other afflicted people.

Even those individuals and non-profit organizations dedicated to helping the refugees, recognize that we cannot open our borders to every African seeking a better life. Millions of Africans have succeeded in reaching Europe. With all the wars, poverty and unrest plaguing their continent, millions more might be interested in giving Israel a try.

"Let's send them to another African country where they'd fit in better," is one suggestion. But which country would agree to take the refugees Israel doesn't want? Even extremely poor countries such as Chad are overrun with refugees already.

"Send them back to Egypt," others urge. "They already had a life for themselves there. They're not really refugees."

Israel's Prime Minister Ehud Olmert has not been sympathetic toward the refugees' plight. He supposedly reached an agreement with President Hosni Mubarak from Egypt that any Sudanese returned to Egypt from Israel would be treated well and not returned to Sudan. The new policy was tested a few days later when a group of 48 refugees were caught trying to cross into Israel and sent right back to Egypt. We heard stories from our Sudanese friends that five of them were returned to Sudan and some were killed.

As more African refugees continue to arrive in Israel, the dilemma and complications grow. How can economic refugees, those fleeing poverty, be distinguished from political refugees?

*E*ven with Father Bent's strenuous efforts, it took six months for us to be released. I really praised God on that day! At the end of June 1998 we were taken to the Meheba refugee camp on the border of Angola.

In the camp we met a wonderful man, Getachew from Ethiopia, who was working for a refugee organization called Care International. Getachew had run away from Mengistu, the Ethiopian dictator, to avoid being killed. He fled to Canada where he studied agriculture, and later came to Zambia as the director of that camp. Getachew was an excellent administrator and a wonderful person.

We arrived in Meheba on a chilly night. June, you know, is winter in southern Africa. It's the opposite type of climate from Sudan. So it was amazing to me. I'd read about these things, but I couldn't believe it when I saw it.

Gabriel started laughing again. Apparently the difference in climate struck him as hilarious.

Getachew was sitting in a club outside the fence drinking with his friends. When we came through the outer gate, he spotted us from far away. Having been informed that three Sudanese were on the way, he recognized us.

'Are you Sudanese?' he asked in English, then introduced himself as the camp's manager. I recognized his Ethiopian accent.

'I've heard about your suffering and that you were in prison,' he said. 'Your country is really in a mess. One thing I am willing to do to help you—it's up to you—is to send you to school. Can you tell me your educational background? Do you have your school certificates? I need to see those papers.'

'We were in a school,' I told him. 'But they weren't formal schools. They were refugee schools. We were learning under the trees. Maybe you can take us to the nearby school for them to test us and place us in the right level.'

He agreed and said that if we worked very hard at the school, he would support us. So after three days we went to Mayever High School, a school for refugees from grade eight to grade twelve.

We found the headmaster, Mambula, from the western area of Zambia, to be a very kind man. When we spoke to him he listened and was interested.

'Okay now, your English is good,' he said to us. 'Tell me in which grade should I put you? Each one of you can choose.'

'We don't have junior certificates; therefore we shouldn't go to senior,' I told him. 'I was in grade six in Kakuma refugee camp in Kenya. Therefore I can start grade eight here. And the coming year I'll sit for the junior-leaving certificate. If I succeed, I'll advance to high school.'

Mambula was happy with my suggestion and the three of us enrolled in grade eight in the junior school. The following year we all passed the exam and went on to the senior high school. We continued studying until I finished grade twelve in high school at the end of 2001. I was about twenty four years old.

Life was difficult in the camp, but Getachew encouraged us to stick to our studies.

'That's your only hope,' he told us. 'If you work hard now, then in the future, if you return to Sudan, you'll be able to support yourselves and your families.'

Getachew was a good, honest man but he had a complicated job and encountered many problems with many of the other refugees. Discouraged, he eventually resigned, incited by a Zambian who didn't want him to be manager. Our camp suffered a great loss when he and his wife went to Lusaka to open a fueling station.

Then we had another problem. The new director and other people were against us. 'Now your protector is gone,' he told us. 'We cannot continue helping you.'

Everything changed after that. I was forced to stop my studies. Although I wasn't allowed to leave the camp according to my UN document, I was able to contact Getachew again, transfer to a technical school, and complete my education.

After finishing school I wasn't allowed to remain in Zambia but was persuaded to return to Kenya or possibly to Sudan. I realized that to be accepted to a Zambian university would take time, and working was out of the question.

A British teacher, who had previously worked in south Sudan, encouraged me. 'Much of southern Sudan is safe. I believe you'll be okay there.'

I was headed home, excited about finding my mother and the rest of my family.

Is anyone still alive? I wondered.

Nairobi, Khartoum and Cairo

I am amazed at the mobility of the Africans. With no passport Gabriel traveled through Sudan, Ethiopia, Kenya, Tanzania and Zambia. We met one man who had been in Israel only a few days.

Tom, our son-in-law, asked him, "How long were you in Egypt?"

"Two days," he replied.

"What? Only two days? How's that possible?" Tom and our daughter Moriah lived among the Sudanese on Kibbutz Eilot and were familiar with their stories. Almost all the Sudanese we knew had been in Egypt for four, five, even ten years.

"Five years ago I ran away from the war in Darfur and came to Libya," he explained. "I was living there until a week ago when I spoke on the phone to a friend. 'You should come to Israel,' he told me. 'I'm working here in the kibbutz and the life is pretty good.' So I got on a bus, passed through Egypt, and three days later reached the border with Israel. Bedouins guided me to the border and now I'm here."

*A*fter making my decision to return to Sudan and seek my relatives, I worked a bit to pay for the train ticket. I traveled through Nairobi and continued north to the border at Lokichokio (the place where we Lost Boys entered Kenya in 1991) before going to my home village.

I searched for my mother and met her for the first time since 1987. She was alone because all seven of us children were scattered. She told me how Arab militias killed my father in an attack on our village. Now she was doing some farming and I helped her watch our few remaining cows.

I was surprised how dispassionately Gabriel described his father's murder as well as meeting his mother whom he hadn't seen in fifteen years.

Had his refugee experience dulled his emotions, perhaps out of necessity in order not to ache continually? Or was this just Gabriel's way of relating an event that was painful to describe? And what about his mother? She must have been dreaming about this day for years, not even knowing if he was alive.

*A*t sunrise one morning our village was attacked. I was arrested along with several other young men and taken to the town of Bor. It was June 2002. The military officers accused me of being a rebel soldier and tortured me and the others horribly.

'Confess!' they demanded. 'And we'll stop beating you.'

'I have nothing to confess,' I told them. 'I'm not a rebel. I'm just helping my mother on our farm.'

'You're lying!' they said and imprisoned me for one month.

Finally realizing I had nothing to do with the rebels, they released me and transferred me to Khartoum on condition that I report regularly to the authorities. Thankfully, the peace process was in progress at that time and both sides showed more under-standing and flexibility.

'We shouldn't kill people while we're on the negotiating table,' they told each other. 'Especially someone like this who had no guns and was just looking after his cows.'

I stayed for a year in Khartoum, but the police came regularly to my home, questioning and threatening me. I worked but I wasn't free; my movements were restricted. At that time the war in Darfur erupted and they were even accusing me of collaborating with the Darfurians, a ridiculous charge. I was arrested and released several times.

When I saw that my life was really in danger, I turned to my uncle. 'I will help you, but because of my position here, no one should know I'm your uncle,' he told me. 'Let it seem as if you're being helped by the church. I'll give money to the pastor and he'll organize your trip to Cairo where you'll meet other Sudanese. You can submit your application to the UN there and perhaps you'll have a chance of resettlement.'

Under constant surveillance, I had difficulty leaving Khartoum, but I finally made my escape. I traveled by train to Wadi Halfa on the Egyptian border and from there by steamer down the Nile to Aswan. I took mini-buses to Cairo.

I arrived in Cairo on June 17, 2004. After a week I went to the UN office, submitted the details of my case, and began the process to obtain official refugee status. Eventually they told me, 'Go to the Ministry of the Interior and they will give you temporary residence.'

I quickly discovered that life in Egypt was so difficult. Even finding something to eat was a struggle. The only support for the Sudanese came from churches, so I volunteered in the church school as an English and Dinka language teacher. The church was our source of comfort, spiritual strength, and also provision for many of our physical needs. We especially loved celebrating our south Sudanese holidays like Christmas and Easter.

After completing a three month course at the American University as a Dinka/English interpreter, I began working for the UN and the IOM, the International Office for Migration, which oversees refugees being resettled to America.

Though financially I was better off, I couldn't escape harassment from the Sudanese Embassy who sent agents to spy on us.

The Sudanese Embassy hired Arabs, especially Nubians from Aswan, to attack us. If you were on the way home from church or even just walking on the road they would assault you because of your color and for being a Christian.

With the Sudanese agents as well as Egyptians persecuting and killing our people, we organized ourselves for protection and encouragement. I was vice-chairman of our state's refugee youth movement.

'Don't move at night or you may be killed,' I advised the young people. 'And stick together so if anything happens you can support one another until the police come.'

When we asked UN officials about our cases, the officials told us, 'The peace process is going on in south Sudan. When everything is okay, you can go back.' But, meanwhile, refugees were being persecuted and killed daily.

We mobilized ourselves and made a sort of hunger strike near the UN office, from September 2005 until the police assault in December. Nothing changed. We contacted Geneva, the UN headquarters. No one helped. Since the UN failed to solve our immediate problems, the Egyptian government took action.

On December 30, 2005 we were peacefully demonstrating and demanding our rights, when thousands of armed police struck many of us, killing men, women and children. The Egyptians claim that twenty six people were killed in this confrontation, but we know the number was much higher.

From then on they cracked down even more on those they suspected of being leaders. My job was traveling from prison to prison with UN officials to interpret for Sudanese who had been captured. But even leaving my house was dangerous.

After all I've been through, why should I lose my life for nothing here in Egypt? I thought.

Israel seemed my best option. Actually I felt I had no choice— Egypt was impossible; I couldn't return to Sudan as long as the present government was in charge, and no other land would accept me. I decided to take a chance on the country inscribed in my passport as the only land we Sudanese were forbidden to visit.

I knew crossing the border was extremely dangerous and that even in Israel life might be hard. In my heart, though, I felt peace, because already in Africa I knew about the Promised Land. We identified with the children of Israel and their desire to escape from slavery to freedom. We likened John Garang, our liberator, to Moses. John Garang read regularly the Old and New Testaments and God inspired him. He was known for praying for guidance from the Lord and for those who came to him with problems.

All of us Sudanese knew about Isaiah 18. We knew this chapter was talking about Sudan, because when Isaiah writes 'beyond the rivers of Ethiopia' (Isaiah 18:1), the word in Hebrew is 'Cush' which means the area of north Sudan. Verse 2 speaks about 'vessels of reeds' and everyone knows that we are the only people who use this kind of boat. Of course Sudan is the 'land the rivers divide,' because the White and Blue Niles meet in what is Khartoum today.

We Dinkas as well as other south Sudanese tribes are among the tallest people in Africa and in verse 7 it is written, 'tall and smooth of skin,' because we don't have much hair on our bodies, not like you white people.

And finally it is written, 'a people feared far and wide,' or in another translation, 'a terrible people.' We Sudanese like to fight and are more aggressive than other African people groups. In the old times we used to fight among ourselves, like the Nuer against the Dinka, but we always maintained our boundaries. The clashes never got out of hand until we acquired automatic rifles and were set against each other by the British and then the Arabs.

So you can see how this chapter exactly fits us. In Sudan we were familiar with this prophecy that the Sudanese would go to Israel to bring a present 'to the Lord of hosts ... to Mount Zion' (verse 7). But in reality I never dreamed I would see that day. What chance did I, a former citizen of a radical Muslim state but now a refugee with no passport, have of going to Israel? Even in our times of the greatest difficulties and suffering, we never lost hope of one day entering heavenly Jerusalem. But setting my feet in earthly Jerusalem seemed as likely as walking on the moon.

Thus when I felt the noose tightening around my neck in Cairo, Israel came to my mind. I knew it wasn't my plan but God's, and I immediately took action.

I already told you about my crossing into Israel and the year I stayed in prison.

What we love about the prophecy in Isaiah 18 is that the Sudanese pointed it out to us. We didn't read these verses and try to force them to fit the situation of the refugees today. No wonder they were so excited when we took them to Jerusalem for Christmas. They believed that when they stood on Mount Zion they were actually fulfilling Isaiah 18. Undoubtedly, however, the final fulfillment will come in the future when the Messiah returns to his Holy City.

Epilog

Gabriel remained in Eilat for three months working at the

Royal Beach Hotel. He was a big help to us—whenever a Sudanese came who couldn't speak English, we called Gabriel and he would either come or talk to them on the phone. During those months after May 2007, when the wave of Sudanese refugees jumping over the border was the strongest, Gabriel was our translator and go-between. The refugees needed help with clothes, medical help, child care, housing and employment. John and I tried to help them.

In fact, in the eyes of the Sudanese, Abuna (John) could do anything. For instance, one day a young woman came to our home with a friend who spoke a little English.

"How can I help you?" John asked.

"I want a baby," she answered seriously.

John was stunned. This request was a new one. "Am I God that I can give you a baby?" he joked, trying to understand what his role was meant to be. Later he realized she was asking him to pay for infertility treatments.

As much as I enjoyed my friendship with John and Judy and the people in the Shelter and being able to assist the new Sudanese refugees, I didn't feel that hotel work was for me.

The situation was complicated, because when we were released from jail we were bound to work for one employer. But someone who works for the Organization for Migrant Workers took my case and found me a job on a farm, working with sheep. So three months after arriving in Eilat, I moved to Moshav Bar Giora outside of Jerusalem. With agriculture my chosen profession, I believed working on a farm would help advance my education.

Then the law changed, and we refugees were transferred from the Ministry of Defense to the Ministry of the Interior and were given more freedom of movement. That allowed me to choose where I wanted to work. I stayed in Jerusalem and studied Hebrew, worked in a gardening shop, and spent time with my fiancée, who I met in Ketziot Prison. She's also from south Sudan.

I attended an *ulpan*, a Hebrew school where we studied every morning for five hours over a period of four months. I believe it's important to learn the language of the local society.

Since coming out of prison I've been involved in trying to form an organization to unite the Sudanese in Israel. With many needs, the first of which is achieving a permanent status, it's imperative that we present a united front in our meetings with the Israeli government and the UN. I believe we must speak with one voice and have one agenda. We have at least four groups who claim to represent us. I'm not talking about the Darfurians, because they have their own council. At one point we thought to organize in a democratic manner—each of the ten states in south Sudan would have two representatives—but it hasn't worked. I believe this diminishes our chances of achieving our purposes, but what can I do? I still have hope, but it's not easy.

Gabriel didn't give up his desire to study in university and applied to Hebrew University for their "preparation course." He was accepted, a miracle in itself, but the expense for a foreign student was prohibitive. However, when a couple of customers from the gardening shop where he worked heard about Gabriel's problem, impressed undoubtedly by his intelligence and determination, they chose to sponsor his tuition. We're very proud of Gabriel, one of the only refugees studying in an Israeli university.

I admire Gabriel's perseverance and absolute trust in God. His life has led him on extreme journeys not of his own choosing. Having to leave all his family as a young boy, he faced death innumerable times. In Israel his life is more physically and materially secure, but he still cannot plan his future. Though content to be in Israel, Gabriel understands the Israeli government doesn't accept him. And in his heart he longs to return to Sudan.

Where will Gabriel be next year? Or even next month? I wonder. One thing I know—my life is richer since Gabriel stepped through our front gate.

2. Muna Maria

Muna Maria and her youngest child

Abducted

"Wow, what a story I just heard," John announced over lunch. "There's a new family in the Shelter—Andrew and his wife Muna. You'll have to meet them. Muna doesn't speak English, but Andrew knows it well. He told me that, as a little girl, Muna was abducted by an Arab from her home in south Sudan and taken to the north."

"Invite them over," I said. "I'm collecting stories like that. People here in Israel and abroad need to hear about these things."

Three evenings prior, John had received a call on his cell phone. "Hello Abuna," a man with a Sudanese accent began. "This is Bol, from the Red Rock Hotel. I've been to the Friday meetings in the Shelter. I'm calling because I was hoping you could help me. Three families, my relatives, just came to me from Egypt. They crossed the border last night. They're with three children too, and I only have a small room with two beds. Could they come to you in the Shelter?"

"Sure," John replied to Bol. "Bring them up. I have three rooms free."

Thankfully it was a quiet period in the hostel.

John was used to receiving such calls—day or night. In May 2007, the wave of Sudanese refugees began pouring into Israel. By June fifty or more men, women, children and babies were crossing the border from Egypt into Israel every day. (*USA TODAY*, August 19, 2007).They passed over the rugged territory in the night, often under fire from Egyptian soldiers, carrying nothing except the clothes they were wearing.

In the beginning the calls to John weren't usually asking for lodging in our Shelter Hostel. The dozens of hotels in Eilat, Israel's southern resort on the Red Sea, were eager for cheap labor, and the Sudanese who reached Eilat were able to move immediately into housing for the hotel workers.

Dafna, the coordinator for the Sudanese on Kibbutz Eilot where hotel workers lived, would call John. "We just received thirty new refugees who came right from the border. They don't have any clothes and the children have no toys."

"Don't worry," John reassured her. "I'll be there soon."

John first made a few phone calls to friends, including those with young children. "There are thirty new Sudanese in Kibbutz Eilot. They need clothes and toys for their children desperately."

Then he went into our room. It looked to me like John had simply moved the whole contents of his closet into plastic bags.

"But you've only got two T-shirts left now," I protested weakly. "And that shirt, the one Jojo from Nigeria gave you years ago, how can you give that away?"

But John didn't think twice—everything went to the refugees.

I, meanwhile, carefully picked out several items I hadn't worn lately. Later I delighted to meet some of the girls and women looking elegant in my blouses and skirts.

By the time Andrew and Muna arrived in Israel with the other two families, the hotels weren't hiring as quickly any more. Families particularly had proved too complicated and costly for them in terms of the social and health services required. The social worker from one of the hotel chains was suddenly swamped with work and had begun working twelve hour days.

Andrew, Muna and friends ended up staying with us for a couple of months while waiting for their UN refugee documents. At that point they were able to officially work and John moved them into studio apartments he rented in another hostel.

When Muna and Andrew stepped into our house for the first time, holding their two small children, my first thought was, *Wow, is she beautiful!* Like many Dinka men and women, she was tall and thin, about 5'8" (172 cm). Straight-backed, she made me think of an African princess. Her dyed reddish hair was braided in an artistic pattern. Yet with an engaging smile and friendly, slanting eyes, Muna didn't give the impression of being vainly aware of her striking looks.

After the usual greetings and shared cups of tea and cookies, I began speaking with Andrew. Muna meanwhile, had pulled her breast out of her dress as I'd discovered was common among the Sudanese, and was unselfconsciously nursing her baby.

"My wife was taken from her family when she was a little girl," Andrew began. "She'd like to tell you her story, but doesn't speak English. I found her and know her story well, so I'll tell it as if she was speaking. Her given name was unknown until recently, but her Arabic name is Muna, which she grew up using."

So Andrew, with their two-year-old nestled on his lap, began speaking while glancing periodically at his wife and stopping to ask her questions.

*T*he only details I know about my family and my early childhood are the things that have been told to me. I was born in Wau in south Sudan, the daughter of Simon Madeng and Adak, my mother. Before the war, Wau was one of the three largest cities in south Sudan, along with Juba and Malakal. My father, as most Dinkas, worked as a farmer, but he also worked for the government as an accountant. My mother took care of the children and the household.

I have absolutely no memories from my life in Wau. Until 2005, when I was twenty four years old, I didn't even know my real name. I'm learning, but I still can't properly speak Dinka, my mother tongue, our tribal language.

When I was six or seven years old I was abducted by a man named Sid Ahmed, who was from north Sudan. At that time, he was stationed as a military officer nearby because the government from Khartoum was fighting south Sudan. That war caused horrible destruction to our people and our land. Millions of people were killed, wounded and made into refugees.

I've often wondered how that man caught me. Was I the only little girl around or did he pick me out of a group of children? What would my life have been like if I hadn't been kidnapped? What would it have been like to grow up in south Sudan with my real family? I don't know if it is caused by the trauma, but my mind is completely blank. I can't even remember my reaction or feelings at the time of my abduction, but I'm sure I was petrified, especially after I realized that the stranger who had grabbed me wasn't taking me home.

Years later, when I found my birth family, my older sister and brother filled in the details of how it happened. I was in my sister's house at the time. She was inside preparing food and I was playing outside. My mother came that afternoon to visit my sister. People always went to visit family and friends at that time, before the 6:00 P.M. curfew when all roads closed.

After my mother went home, suddenly a huge fire began burning in the mango plantation near our house. Not far from where we lived was an SPLA (Sudanese People's Liberation Army) garrison, and the government soldiers were always suspicious and didn't trust the civilians. They thought the civilians were aiding the SPLA rebels. These clashes were happening all over south Sudan. The government would set whole villages on fire. And so, on the day I was taken, the government soldiers began shooting in our direction and the mango grove caught on fire. Homes and shops burned down. It sounds horrifying when I think about it now.

So when the blaze broke out in our village, all the children began running in different directions. They didn't know where to go—they saw no way out. I was one of those frightened children. And that's when a soldier grabbed me and took me away.

I wonder: Did he see a scared, crying little girl and want to help me? But why then didn't he try to find my family after the fire died down? Why did he take me far from my village and my people?

Later I heard that when the flames cooled, my sister and mother began frantically looking but couldn't find me. Did the soldier immediately take off with me for the north in his car, or did he hide me in his room? We will never know. Other children were also lost in that fire. It must have been chaos in our village—parents looking for their children and children who had run too far away and couldn't find their way home.

My family was desperate because they knew the government forces were in the habit of stealing girls especially. On the other hand, some of them decided that I was most likely killed by one of the Arab soldiers. I was told that after that day, my mother was never the same. But she also never gave up looking for her little girl.

Sid Ahmed took me back to his home. He was very rich and had many houses—in Nyala, Port Sudan, Darfur and Khartoum. He had nine children from only one wife, unlike many Muslims who had up to four wives.

At that time, many children were stolen from their families in south Sudan and taken as slaves to the north. Although slavery is an inhumane institution and has been outlawed all over the world, in Sudan thousands of innocent people have been captured and work as slaves even in this day and age.

I could have been one of those enslaved, abused children, but in God's mercy my captor had a kind side. True, he seized me from my family and stole my identity, but afterwards he was kind to me. He brought me into his family and loved me as his own daughter. He never told me that I had been stolen. I don't remember it, but of course no one was able to speak Dinka with me, so I learned to speak Arabic. And he gave me a new name—Muna.

I called Sid Ahmed 'Baba' and his wife 'Mama.' And I used to ask, 'Why do I look different from the rest of the family? I am so black and you are all white.'

'Don't worry,' he answered me. 'Your great-great grand-mother was from the south. She was black like you. That's why your skin is black. You look like her.'

I trusted him and never questioned that story. I was little and just believed what I was told.

One thing I remember is when Sid Ahmed took me to my first day of school. The headmaster asked for my documents. Some-how, and now I wonder how, Sid Ahmed produced some papers. But the name on my birth certificate was 'Muna Mohammed-Ahmed.' The Arabs use the name of Mohammed a lot, including variations like Ahmed and Hammed, but even so I could see that my name wasn't the same as the rest of the family.

I asked, 'Baba, why do I have a different name than you and my brothers and sisters?'

'Don't worry,' he said. But he didn't answer my question. When I was older I wondered if he was thinking about the inheritance he would give to his nine children and didn't want to include me. I don't know.

My school was in the Arabic language, of course. I learned how to read the Koran very well, but we didn't study English at all. The Arabs didn't want anyone to learn English. Many of the schools in the south used to be run by missionaries and were in the English language. But later the government from Khartoum ousted the missionaries, closed their schools, and ordered all education to be in Arabic.

So I was living happily with my father until 1996. I lived like a child in his house and felt his love for me.

'My daughter, my daughter,' he used to say to me.

But then Sid Ahmed became ill. He suffered from heart disease as well as diabetes. So he was taken from Port Sudan where we were living at the time, to a hospital in Khartoum. I didn't even know he was sick because no one told me. But one by one, family members left to go to stay with him in the hospital. In the end, I was left alone there on the farm in Port Sudan. I was about fifteen years old.

When he was in the hospital he told his family, 'I want to see my Muna. Let her come to me so I can tell her the truth.'

'No,' his wife answered. 'She's still so young. She wouldn't understand. Wait until you're well and then talk to her.'

Gradually Sid Ahmed's condition worsened and he was transferred to another hospital. Soon after that he died. The whole family was in mourning. One of my aunts brought me the tragic news.

In the beginning I continued to live with the family and it appeared that things would continue as they had before. It seems to me that even after Sid Ahmed died, people were still afraid of him and knowing how much he loved me, they left me alone and didn't mistreat me.

After two years the time came to take my school exams.

'Mother,' I asked. 'Can you please give me my birth certificate so I can sit for my exams?' Again, as when I registered for first grade, I needed documentation.

'No!' she answered. 'You don't have a proper birth certificate. You'll have to stop your education.'

I was shocked. *What is she talking about?* I thought.

My mother continued, 'You are one of those lost children. While my husband was alive, I wanted to reveal that you are a Dinka, but he became angry with me.'

'If you tell her that secret I'll divorce you!' he said.

'That's why I never told you the truth,' she said. 'But now he's gone and you don't belong here. You are wasting your time if you stay with us. Anyone can come and say they've been stolen and try to steal away my husband's inheritance. But my Sid Ahmed's property belongs to his own children, not to you. Go back to the south where you belong!'

His children, whom up to that point I looked at as my brothers and sisters, said to me, 'You aren't our sister. Our father found you in Wau during the war. You've been brought here in our father's service. How can you stay with us and try to share our father's properties?'

Only sixteen years old, I was helpless and completely at their mercy. Till then I'd been dependent on my father, but now the only one who had loved and protected me was dead. My life completely changed to misery.

By this time the whole family was scattered, living in Port Sudan, Khartoum, Darfur and Saudi Arabia. My step-mother was a sickly woman; she suffered often from diarrhea. When I was around her, my job was washing and cleaning up after her.

The oldest son took me to Nyala in Darfur as his servant where I lived in a shack in the garden. All day long I worked hard in his palm plantation and took care of the cattle and goats. I hardly received any food to eat. No one spoke a kind word to me. The one who had been my brother was now mistreating and exploiting me.

What will my future be? I wondered. *How long can I go on like this?* I dreamed about escaping.

Muna pulled her blouse down from her shoulder. "Look," she said, "you can see the marks where they beat me."

From the favored daughter of a wealthy man, Muna had become a virtual slave to her cruel step-brother. Not only that; she didn't know her real name, language or age.

A Miraculous Reunion

Hearing Muna's story, I realized she was "lucky" to have been taken as a daughter into her kidnapper's family and not used as a sex slave. Nevertheless, Sid Ahmed robbed Muna of her identity, of her self.

Slavery still exists in Sudan. Although the government claims that rival tribes are simply engaged in hostage-takings over which the central government has no control, international organizations such as Human Rights Watch claim there are at least eight thousand slaves currently held in Sudan (BBC News, March 5, 2008). Unlike Britain which outlawed slavery over two hundred years ago, and the United States in 1865, the Sudan Criminal Code has no prohibition against slavery.

Slavery unfortunately is not a new phenomenon in Sudan but has existed for centuries. Raiding for slaves was common under the Turkish-Egyptian rule in the 19th century, when northern Sudan held tens of thousands of slaves and exported thousands more to Egypt and the Arab states. The practice, however, had nearly died out by the 1970s and slave raids were unknown. It surfaced again, however, with Jaafar Numeiri's assumption of the presidency in 1983 and his imposition of the sharia (Islamic religious) law.

The state of chaos engendered by the civil war between the Christian and animist south against the Muslim north which began at that time, created a hospitable environment for slave-taking. Furthermore, Numeiri's government actually encouraged the practice, using slave raids and slavery as an instrument to break resistance against its policies. The government sent Arab Muslim militiamen southwards and allowed them to keep whatever booty they could seize, including the women and children.

*I*n 2003, the war in Darfur broke out. The conditions in our area grew impossible, with fighting, killings, hunger and anarchy. People were fleeing in every direction. I knew this was my opportunity to run away. One of our cousins encouraged me to go and gave me some money. So I joined the stream of refugees and decided to travel to Khartoum and seek my real family. I boarded one of the trains that was still running.

I arrived alone in the enormous city of Khartoum. Hundreds of thousands of displaced persons from the south were living in shantytowns outside the city. I remembered that my step-mother had told me that my father, Sid Ahmed, took me from the town of Wau. My goal was to find someone in Khartoum who could give me a clue about my identity.

I met a woman who gave me some food and told me that a black woman like me could work as a servant. I was desperate, but I soon discovered that she worked in prostitution, so I didn't stay with her.

I met two south Sudanese girls who lived with their parents.

They were kind, and I could stay with them. When I told them that I was looking for my family, they informed me that the Minister of Agriculture, the highest Dinka in the government, was originally from Wau. His family had once been Christian, but anyone who wanted a high position in the regime was forced to convert to Islam.

I sought him out and this Minister offered to take me into his house. I knew that he had many connections and went to events where there were people from Wau. I hoped he would ask if there was anyone who had lost a little girl around the time I was abducted. And this way I would find my true family.

Unfortunately this Minister had other ideas. After a while I discovered that he wasn't doing anything to help find my origins.

Rather, he began to tell people, "This girl in my house, she's the one whose life I saved. She belongs to me."

He even told people that I was his daughter.

I understood that all he wanted was to get me married and collect the dowry. But I knew he was lying: he wasn't my father and he didn't save me.

With her stunning appearance, I could imagine that many suitors would have come to ask for Muna's hand, and that the Minister correctly reckoned he could demand a high bride price for her.

What a frightening position for a young woman—alone in the huge city with no protector—especially in the Arab culture where a woman lived under the guardianship of her father until she married and then belonged to her husband. Muna had no one to help her, none of her people who even knew of her existence.

For three months I lived in the Minister's home. When he finally arranged a marriage for me and I refused, he threw me out of the house.

But God was working in a way I couldn't have imagined. Meanwhile I had met Andrew, a friend of the Minister's son who lived nearby with his uncle. One time when he came over to the house, he asked me about my family.

'Who were your parents? From what clan and tribe do you come?' he wanted to know.

'I don't know anything of my background,' I answered. 'I was abducted when I was little and taken to the north by an Arab. I can't remember anything, but the woman who was my step-mother told me I'm from Wau. Now I've run away from those people and am looking for my real family. That's why I came to the house of this Minister. I believed he'd help me find parents, brothers and sisters, but he's only telling lies and trying to get me married.'

I had often seen Andrew when he came to visit and felt I could trust him.

'You can stay with us in my uncle's house,' he said. 'And I want to help you find your family. You are so beautiful, that when you get your family back, I'll marry you. Even if you don't discover your family, I'll still marry you. But I'd like for you to be educated and receive a graduation certificate.'

After the terrible disappointment of staying with that Minister, I finally had hope again. I found someone who cared about me. Andrew was different from other men I'd met.

He told me he was a Christian. 'Your family in Wau must have been Christian too,' he said. 'And I can only marry a Christian woman.'

'I don't know anything about the Christian faith,' I said. 'I've been raised as a Muslim. We heard that Christians are unclean and the Bible is full of lies.'

Andrew gave me a Bible in Arabic and a booklet explaining the differences between the Bible and the Koran. I had studied the Koran for years and could read it very well, but I'd never opened the Bible in my life. I began eagerly reading it and realized that the Koran contained many quotes and stories from the Bible, but they hadn't been translated correctly.

I'd been taught, as all good Muslims are, that Abraham took Ishmael to the mountain in Jerusalem to sacrifice him. We even have a feast to celebrate this occasion, the Eid el Adha. But in the

Bible I read that it was Abraham's son Isaac. I believed that the
Jews and the Christians had perverted the Bible and that the Koran
was God's final and pure revelation to us. Mohammed, according
to the Koran, was God's last prophet.

Which was true, I wondered, the Bible or the Koran?

The Koran spoke about Jesus, but presented a very different
picture of Him than the Bible did. As a Muslim I was taught that
if our good deeds outnumbered our bad deeds, we would receive
favor in God's eyes and merit a place in heaven. But in the Bible
I read that through faith in Jesus alone we receive forgiveness
for our sins.

In the beginning I was confused, because I'd attended schools
for eight years where the Koran was taught. But the more I read
the Bible, the more I found myself believing that Jesus was the
true way. In the gospel of John it says, 'I am the way, the truth,
and the life.' Now I could recognize that there was no one else
like Him in all of history.

'I've made my decision,' I told Andrew. 'I want to be a
Christian and follow Jesus. I'm not a Muslim any more.'

After that we were married. We had a traditional ceremony,
but Andrew's family had no one to give the dowry to, because I
had no family. Our traditional weddings begin with the important
people from our tribe sitting together and drinking our homemade
wine. This is made from grain and is like porridge which we
then filter.

Because we weren't in our tribal area we didn't wear the
traditional leather clothes but rather Western wedding clothes.
Andrew and I entered the room for only about ten minutes with
simple vows, in which we agreed that he would take care of
me and I would live peaceably with him. The elders continued
drinking and dancing and later handed over the dancing to the
younger people who continued until early morning. That was our
wedding.

I was happier than I'd ever been in my life—especially when
some time later, I found I was pregnant. I still hadn't located my
family and after all the years of war in south Sudan, I didn't know

if they were even alive. But I had hope I'd find them someday and now I was starting a new family of my own.

We were living in Khartoum and there's a Turkish hospital there where I went for check-ups during my pregnancy. I noticed that the nurse, also a Sudanese woman from the south, acted strangely towards me.

I would come home from my monthly check-ups and say to Andrew, 'I don't know what this woman wants. She looks at me in a funny way and I feel like she's following me around. I'm unhappy with this lady.'

'Don't worry,' Andrew reassured me. 'It's important you have these check-ups. That woman probably just wants the best for you.'

When I was there for my appointment in the seventh month, I finally said to the nurse, 'Why do you treat me like this?'

'I didn't want to tell you before,' she answered, 'because I was afraid of making a mistake. But you look very much like another woman I knew. She lived with me for three years here in Khartoum looking for her lost daughter whom she believed was stolen by an Arab many years ago from their home in Wau.'

I was shocked and felt light-headed. Was it possible?

'Where's this woman now?' I burst out, almost afraid to hear the answer.

'After three years of looking daily, she was brokenhearted and went back to her home in south Sudan,' the nurse said. 'But I'll call her daughter who lives outside of Khartoum.'

My heart was thumping as the nurse picked up the phone and dialed. After the usual polite greetings she came to the point. 'I'm sitting in the clinic with a woman who looks just like your mother. I know you had a sister who was abducted and was wondering if this could be her. Here, speak to her.'

I took the phone in my shaking hands and heard a voice that was possibly my sister. 'I'm coming right away,' she told me.

As Andrew and I waited at home, I stood up, sat down again, and looked out the door repeatedly. This sister lived north of Khartoum and it took her three hours to reach us in a taxi. When she walked in the door we fell into each other's arms and began crying tears of joy after all the years we'd been separated. We both realized we even looked like each other. Our voices were similar.

'What about the rest of the family, our parents?' I asked.

'Mother was looking for you here in Khartoum for three years. She died not long after returning home to Wau. Father died earlier. But now I want to call our brother who lives in Australia. He was with you when you were taken.'

'I've found our Aleuthin!' my sister announced on the phone to our brother.

My brother wasn't so easily convinced—maybe because he didn't see me standing in front of him.

'There's one way to know if she's really our sister,' he said. 'Aleuthin was wounded on her right ear in an accident when she was little and was left with a scar. You must check to see if this woman who's with you has a scar on her ear.'

My sister gently pulled my braids back from my right ear, and when she saw a scar, we began weeping again, pausing to smile at each other between our sobs. God had done a miracle and reunited me with my family.

Into and Out of Egypt

Muna's story reminded me of the Hidden Children. Living in Israel we hear many stories of children, grown up now, who lost their identities in the Holocaust. Parents passed babies out of windows of trains on the way to concentration camps or handed their little boys and girls to anyone they thought could care for them. Children who were fair and could pass as non-Jews were able to live openly with foster families by obtaining false identity papers and new names. They quickly learned the prayers and rituals of their Protestant or Catholic protectors, including dozens of Catholic convents. Very young children and babies were particularly easy to hide because they were less likely to reveal their past.

Following the war, Jewish parents often spent months and years searching for the children they had sent into hiding, but unfortunately the search for family often ended in tragedy: the parents discovered their child had perished, or were unable to track him or her; the hidden child found that no one else in his family had survived; certain rescuers refused to release the child to family or to a Jewish organization—in some cases they demanded financial compensation, or they had become attached to the child and felt he or she was their own. I've heard tales of people who spend their life wondering who they really are, when they were born, and which parent they look like.

If Muna hadn't met that nurse in Khartoum, a huge city with over two million inhabitants, she could have been like the children whose faces stare out of the Missing Identity website, child Holocaust survivors trying to find the most basic information about themselves. For the Sudanese, however, no such website exists.

*O*ur son, Ater, was born two months after I found my family. At first I thought I could never be happier. I had two families now—my sister and the brother whom I've still never met, plus Andrew, my loving husband, and our beautiful sweet baby. We even had a special celebration to welcome me back into my family and we slaughtered cows given by Andrew's family for the occasion.

But our life in Khartoum was difficult. We were refugees—displaced persons living far from our home in south Sudan. Andrew wanted to study. His father, an engineer, sent Andrew to missionary schools. He thought his son would also be an engineer; but Andrew's dream was to be a doctor. However, all of Andrew's education had been in English and the schools in Khartoum were in Arabic, so there was no way he could study.

'I think we should move to Egypt,' Andrew told me one day. 'We'll have a better life there.'

Today I ask myself why we thought Egypt would be so good. But Sudan was still in a civil war and as black-skinned Dinkas from the south, we were discriminated against there in Khartoum.

So on November 4, 2006 we began our journey from Khartoum to Cairo. Many Sudanese lived there, and in the beginning Egypt seemed to offer us more possibilities.

After a long and frustrating wait, on August 14, 2007 we finally received a green refugee card from the UN, bestowing on us official refugee status. We happily looked forward to the time when the UN would call us for another interview and give us hope for a better future. We waited and waited, but that call never came. Like many Sudanese in Egypt we became frustrated.

Most of the time Andrew was unable to find a job; when he did find one, he received just 400 Egyptian pounds ($75) a month. We were paying 300 pounds ($55) for our rent, so we only had 100 pounds ($18) left to spend on food for the month. That money lasted us for eight or ten days at the most. The rest of the month we were without food. I don't know how we managed.

On top of that the Egyptians in Cairo treated us horribly. We found that they treated us the same as people from northern Sudan. We had no rights that normal people expect. Life was impossible.

Our only light in Cairo was the church. We went to the Zamelek Church and there we found good people who helped refugees. Every two weeks they distributed food to needy people. Each family received a kilo (2.2 lbs) of rice, lentils and sugar. Still it wasn't enough to sustain us, and we were among the many people waiting in line for the allotment.

We had our faith in the Lord Jesus to sustain us. Andrew and I read the Bible together daily and prayed. I remember a Bible passage Andrew shared which he felt applied to us.

'The children of Israel were also living in Egypt long ago,' he began. Since I still wasn't familiar with the Bible, I enjoyed having Andrew explain God's word to me. 'It began when Joseph, Jacob's youngest son, was sold by his jealous brothers to Midianites who in turn sold him to Potiphar, an Egyptian official. It was hard for him to be so far from his family and to work as a slave, but Joseph trusted in God. Even after being falsely accused and thrown into prison, Joseph was miraculously delivered and went on to become Pharaoh's second-in-command.

'Due to famine, Joseph's brothers and their wives and children, as well as his father, Jacob, eventually came down to live in Egypt too so that they would be provided for. In the beginning it seemed they could make good lives there for themselves. But when a new pharaoh arose who didn't know Joseph, they became slaves for over four hundred years.'

'God didn't forget his people, though, and raised up his servant Moses to be their deliverer. God spoke to Moses and told him to take the children of Israel out of Egypt and back to their promised land, to Israel.'

I was beginning to follow Andrew's line of reasoning. 'I think God is showing us also to escape from Egypt to Israel,' he said.

At first I was surprised, though I knew my husband wasn't afraid to take risks. We'd already made the trip from Khartoum to Cairo.

'But how can we go? It will cost us money and we can barely feed ourselves,' I asked. By this time we had two small boys—Ater, one and a half years old, and Emanuel, a newborn. And although we suffered greatly in Cairo, it would be hard to leave everything behind again.

'I'll work harder,' Andrew answered. 'And if God wants us to go, He'll provide.'

After that Andrew tried to work a lot and after some months managed to save 50 Egyptian pounds. At the same time he shared with many people about our circumstances and began collecting money from here and there until we reached $600.

Sudanese friends of ours told us about Sinai Bedouin who helped refugees cross into Israel. Andrew contacted them and we agreed on the payment. They told us to take the bus from Cairo to El Arish, a city on the Mediterranean Sea south of Gaza. But we knew that in Egypt there are many army checkpoints on the roads where they ask for passengers' identification, so Andrew told them to send a car to take us.

'We have a little baby,' Andrew insisted.

On November 26, 2007 we finally left Cairo. Although I was nervous because I'd heard stories about Egyptian soldiers shooting people as they tried to cross into Israel, I was glad to leave Egypt. We took nothing with us—not even an extra set of clothes. The Bedouins told us we would have to run and shouldn't carry bags.

The Bedouins sat us in the back of their truck and told us to put on Islamic dress. For Andrew they had a long white jalabliya, or gown, and for me a dress and head covering where only my eyes would show.

Andrew refused. 'We're not wearing those Islamic clothes.'

But when we came near the Suez Canal, our guide told us that it would be very dangerous for us without those clothes.

'Put them on,' he said, 'and I'll explain to the soldiers at the roadblocks that you are a Saudi Arabian family on your way home.'

The Bedouins drove us through the desert to the Israel border.

'I'll take the big one. You take the baby,' Andrew said. 'He mustn't cry. If the Egyptian soldiers hear him, they'll capture or shoot us. Every time he starts to fuss, put him to your breast.'

We had no food. I couldn't even buy food for the way, because we gave all our money to the Bedouins. I was pressing the baby to my breast all the time and Andrew hugged our older son, Ater, close to him.

*H*ow desperate parents must be to risk such a journey with little children. Was their life in Cairo so bleak or hopeless? And to constantly breastfeed my baby for hours or even days, I couldn't imagine.

'*W*hen you get to Israel, the soldiers will give you food,' our Bedouin driver reassured us.

All the time we were praying hard. 'God, may nothing happen to us on our journey. Please lead us out of Egypt so we can settle in Israel.'

I remembered the story Andrew told me from the Bible about the children of Israel fleeing Egypt. The Red Sea opened before them, but the Egyptian soldiers were following close behind.

We finally came to a mountainous and rocky place and waited until dark. The Bedouins parked their car and told us that now we would have to go on foot. We walked and ran for four hours carrying our children.

The only thing we had with us was a sling for our baby. Andrew was careful to put our important documents in there—our birth certificates, marriage certificate, and all of Andrew's diplomas and certificates. After leaving El Arish, the Bedouin made us lie down in the back of his truck and covered us with a sheet. I was convinced that Andrew had the pouch with our documents, and he was certain I had it. When we stepped out of the car, we realized it was gone—all our important papers!

'Where's our pouch?' Andrew questioned me.

'Never mind,' the Bedouin said. 'Don't worry. Just go!'

I'm still upset when I think of how he took advantage of us and stole our documents.

'Now you must take off your shoes,' the Bedouin told us when we neared the border. 'Carry them in your hand. Many people have been caught because they were wearing shoes.'

The desert's silence accentuates all sounds. The smallest noise can be heard at a great distance. With shoes one might kick a stone or even start a small landslide.

So we ran barefoot over the sharp rocks, hoping we wouldn't cut our feet. Due to the rugged terrain there was no proper border fence.

The Bedouins went ahead to scout out the best place for our group to pass. As we waited in the pitch black, I rested briefly and caught my breath.

After twenty minutes they returned, pointing. 'Over this way. We cut a piece of the fence, but from here you have to go alone. When you reach the fence, raise it up and go inside. Move quickly!'

I prayed as I'd never prayed before. *Just keep us alive God, and help us get to the other side. Protect our two little boys.*

I prayed even as we tried to lift that fence. It was so difficult! As we drew near, the Egyptian soldiers noticed us and began shooting. My heart was pounding, but I kept running, clutching my baby to my breast.

The Israeli soldiers heard the gunfire and came close to where we were. They shouted at the Egyptians, and later Andrew told me that they yelled, 'Don't shoot these people or we'll shoot you!'

But I was afraid when I saw those soldiers. And I couldn't understand their language. *Who are they?* I wondered. *Will they capture us?*

I managed to keep close to my husband and he told me that the soldiers were speaking English and saying to us, 'Come. Don't be afraid. Don't stop!'

I thanked God they weren't shooting at us, but I was still scared. Everyone in our group ran in different directions. The army launched flares and for a moment, the night turned into day. My husband and I crouched behind a rock with another boy trying to make ourselves invisible. Both the Israeli as well as the Egyptian soldiers were searching for us, the Israelis calling out in that strange language. But we were afraid they were Egyptians, so we didn't leave our hiding place.

We were huddled in that cave for more than an hour. Later I learned that some of our friends had been found quickly by the Israelis and while we were still fearfully concealing ourselves, they were already comfortably seated in the Israeli jeep, drinking and eating.

Flare after flare was discharged into the air and eventually we heard voices close to us. They spoke in gentle tones and Andrew interpreted for me. 'Come. We're Israelis. You're safe now.'

Andrew told me later that he heard one of the soldiers call the other one 'Michael''; he knew that wasn't an Arabic name.

The Israeli soldiers convinced us to step out into the light and to trust them. They took us to their army base and gave us water and food—the first time we'd eaten in days. Standing under the shower and washing off the sand and dirt from the past week, I felt the layers of tension peeling off my body. We rinsed our grimy clothes and the soldiers gave us clean ones to put on.

The men were in one section and the women in another. A nurse brought me and my two babies to the hospital. When she examined them, they cried a little but I didn't have to worry any more about someone hearing them. Then we were led to clean, soft beds.

I couldn't understand the language, but I could read the kind expressions on the soldiers' faces. After days of stress and anxiety, I was able to relax and fell into a deep sleep.

New Land, New Life

Not all refugees are so fortunate as to cross the border in one piece, or at all. In the first seven months of 2008, nineteen Africans were killed trying to escape into Israel. (*Reuters*, Aug. 6, 2008)

In August 2007 Egyptian soldiers killed four Sudanese refugees, beating two of them to death in front of horrified Israeli soldiers. One of the Israeli soldiers speaking in a trembling voice on Israeli television reported that as the refugees approached the border, the Egyptian soldiers began shooting. Two of the men were killed immediately and one was wounded.

By this time the Israeli army had been alerted that infiltrators were coming over the border and they sent a jeep to the location. They arrived just in time to see the fourth man climbing over the fence. One of the Israeli soldiers stretched out his arms in an attempt to help him across but he was pulled back by two Egyptian soldiers. A tug-of-war ensued, each side holding on to the Sudanese. When the Egyptians pointed their guns at the Israelis, the Israeli soldiers let go and then watched helplessly as the Egyptians dragged him and his wounded friend away from the fence and assaulted them with sticks and rocks until they died. (*Jerusalem Post*, Aug. 2, 2007)

In another instance, John met Mohammed, a twenty-some-thing-year-old man from Darfur, at Kibbutz Eilot in the housing for hotel workers. One of our Sudanese friends had suggested that John visit this wounded man. Mohammed spoke passable English and explained to John that he was shot on the border and had three bullets in his leg.

"They took the bullets out in Soroka Hospital in Beer Sheva," he said and gently lifted the sheet off his leg to show his bandages. "Afterwards I came here to stay with my cousin, who arrived in Israel last year."

John was shocked to see the ugly state of Mohammed's leg. The bandages were old and blood-soaked, and yellow pus was oozing out of the wounds.

"We have to get you to a doctor," John said. "I'll help you walk to my car."

"But how can I pay?" Mohammed asked. "Those who work receive a card from the hotel entitling them to health insurance. But I haven't been able to work yet."

"Never mind," John insisted. "This has to be taken care of, if you ever want to walk again."

The admissions clerk at the hospital objected at first, but she finally relented and allowed Mohammed into the emergency room where his leg was cleaned and bandaged and he received heavy doses of antibiotics.

In the coming days he continued to have his dressings changed regularly and eventually had the surgical clips taken out of his leg. Finally Mohammed was taken to a rehabilitation hospital in Tel Aviv for long-term physiotherapy, thankful to be alive and hoping to someday walk normally again, without a pronounced limp.

In contrast, Muna and Andrew's border crossing had a positive ending—they all made it safely and in one piece to Israel.

We knew we wouldn't stay at the army base and wondered what would happen to us next. When evening came, soldiers

arrived and said they would take us to town. They drove us to
Beer Sheva, an hour's drive, and dropped us off near another base,
along with two other families.

'Wait here,' the officer said. 'The police will come and pick
you up.'

We waited in the dark, cold night and we didn't have warm
clothes for our children.

'Let's pray,' Andrew said and he spoke aloud. 'God, show us
what to do now. Send someone to us with a kind heart.'

Then Andrew told the other families, 'Let's walk to the light.
Someone will surely see us and pick us up.'

We began walking and after twenty minutes came to a junc-
tion. Many cars were whizzing past and finally one stopped.

The driver rolled down his window and asked, "What are you
doing here?"

'We're Sudanese,' Andrew answered.

'But why are you standing in the cold and dark with your
little children?'

'We just came over the border from Egypt into Israel,'
Andrew said. 'We don't know where to go and now we're stuck.'

'My name is Manir. Come to my house.'

Manir welcomed us in his home and helped us to call Bol, the
relative of Abraham, one of those in our group. Bol had crossed
the border earlier and was working in Eilat. The first time we
called, Bol didn't answer, but finally he picked up the phone.

'We're here!' Abraham announced to Bol. 'We made it!'

Bol told us he was at work, but that we should try to make
it down to Eilat. Bol spoke to Manir on the phone and asked if
he could drive us.

'I'll pay you when you arrive,' Bol promised.

Manir agreed and we drove through the desert for three hours
to reach Eilat. We went straight to Bol's room, but it was clear
he had no place for all of us. The other families had four and
five people each.

'I'll call Abuna John,' Bol offered. 'He has the Shelter and
likes to help people. I know other Sudanese who've stayed there.'

I was so happy. God had brought us to Israel, into the Promised Land, and I knew He'd take care of us. But till now I had been concerned about finding a safe place for my boys to stay.

'Thank you Jesus!' I felt like shouting.

When I came to the Shelter and met Abuna John, I knew we'd come to the right place. I didn't feel as if we were bothering Abuna at all. He seemed genuinely glad to meet and help us.

The Shelter is larger than a private house and has many rooms. In the center there's a courtyard which is covered at one end with palm branches and has comfortable chairs and sofas and carpets. I felt peace when I stepped in the gate.

Besides Abuna, several other people came to receive us and show us our rooms. Everyone made a fuss over our two boys and quickly took them out of my hands. I was glad to have my arms free, especially after the days spent in the back of that Bedouin truck pressing little Emanuel to my breast for fear he'd cry and we'd all be caught. And although he was light, my arms ached as we trudged through the desert and dashed across the fence.

'You are welcome to stay in the Shelter until you get your UN papers and can begin to support yourselves,' Abuna told us. 'Here you don't have to worry about anything. We'll take care of your food too. Tell me what you like to eat, because Judy, my wife, will go shopping tomorrow.'

That was November 28, 2007 when we arrived in the Shelter, and we stayed until January. We had to wait for the UN representative to interview us and give us permission to work. When Andrew found a job, Abuna John moved us into a hostel with apartments where many Sudanese were living. We were thankful to be able to take responsibility for ourselves, but we continued to go to the meetings at the Shelter.

I pray that all the Sudanese people can live in peace, and that my boys will find a better life than Andrew and I had. I pray that Israel allows us to stay here until peace comes to south Sudan and we can go home.

I've asked myself whether I would have had the courage or the foolishness to cross the border with a baby and a toddler as Muna and Andrew did. But I'll never fully understand the circumstances that drove them to such an extreme decision. The more I come to know Andrew, I see he's a man who seeks the best for his family and is willing to take risks.

I wonder where his risk-taking will eventually lead them: To a better job in Israel? To a third country? Or back to Sudan to help in establishing a new country?

The majority of the Sudanese refugees in Israel are from the south, and they are the ones we've come to know the best. I've read books about their lives and tried to understand the causes of the prolonged civil war in south Sudan that began in 1983. The civilian death toll is said to be one of the highest of any war since World War II.

Yet as we began our involvement with the Sudanese refugees in Israel, Darfur appeared regularly in the news—not south Sudan. Although the war in south Sudan has been called Africa's longest-running war[1], one reason for the lack of news coverage today is the Comprehensive Peace Agreement signed on January 9, 2005 between the SPLA and the government of Sudan.

The peace agreement provides for a regional government with substantial powers in southern Sudan. After six years, in January 2011, a vote took place in which the citizens of south Sudan chose to become independent.

The agreement established an internationally monitored cease-fire and addressed complicated issues such as power sharing in the transitional government, wealth sharing particularly in regard to the huge oil reserves in the south, and the sharia law[2]. Needless to say, the peace agreement is extremely fragile, and violent outbreaks of fighting threaten to destroy the peace.

---

1. http://www.voanews.com/english/archive/2005-01/2005
   -01-07-voa59.cfm
2. http://www.care.org/newsroom/articles/2005/01/
   20050111_sudan_peace_qa.asp

Epilog

"*I* have to tell you something," Andrew began, when John and I visited them in November of 2010. "There's been a change."

He told the story for Muna, who had started remembering some things from her childhood before the abduction.

A few months ago (I don't know why) I was thinking about when I lived in the house of Sid Ahmed. Unexpectedly I remembered a day, long after his death, when his eldest son said to me, 'If you escape from here, you'll never get back to Okacho.'

I had no idea who Okacho was and didn't dare to ask. I just kept planning my escape. But when this memory came to me, Andrew and I resolved that when we returned to Sudan someday, I'd go to that 'big brother' and ask him about Okacho.

Not long after that, Andrew was in Tel Aviv looking for a job. He was with a couple of friends and saw some Sudanese men sitting on a bench.

'I noticed,' he told me, 'that one man had cuts on his forehead the same as yours.'

As you know, many Sudanese have scars, often done as an initiation into adulthood. For us they are signs by which we can tell from which tribe a person comes.

"*I* have three small lines here," Muna said, moving closer to me and pushing aside her braids. Staring hard and squinting, I could barely see her marks, which looked like the shape of the Hebrew letter shin.

"Even Andrew tells me that he didn't notice them until long after we'd started seeing each other."

*A*ndrew asked the man at what age they get these marks in his tribe.

'I'm a Kakwa,' he answered. 'We're a small tribe that originally came from Uganda but now live around Juba. With us, you can get these at any age, often quite young.'

'Do you know of anyone from your tribe who lost a son or daughter?' Andrew asked, his curiosity aroused, but trying to remain calm. At this point, he didn't want to give anything away by mentioning me. That's why he said 'son or daughter.'

'My uncle, Okacho, lost his daughter,' he said.

Okacho isn't a common name, so Andrew was really interested. He questioned the man, named Justin, some more and told him about me, and asked if he would investigate.

'Unfortunately,' he informed Andrew, 'Okacho died in 2006.'

When Andrew came home and told me about this chance meeting, other details of my past started coming back to me. The name of my sister, Bakita, suddenly came into my mind; she had been my best friend. I could visualize our street again and the church we attended.

'He even looks like you,' Andrew said. 'He could be your cousin."

A thick, tightly-closed gate seemed to be slowly cracking open about my past and I remembered that my father had two wives. The one who wasn't my mother didn't like me and now I'm dead sure that she actually sold me to that Arab, Sid Ahmed. I even remembered that my real name was Maria.

Sometimes it's so hard to think about my life and I wonder why all this happened to me. Why did I have to go through all this pain? Why can't I have a real family like other people?

*M*aybe it sounded like a cliché, but all I felt I could do was to put my arm around Muna and remind her that God is her Father and He loves her completely and forever. She was speaking quickly and blinked back a tear. I could hardly fathom how, after one chance meeting Andrew had with a random man on the street, Muna's whole identity had changed.

For me the story of Okacho seemed to raise more questions than it answered.

I gently asked, "But how do you know that this is your real family—not the sister who found you in Khartoum?"

"Now I'm very sure," she answered.

"And why would that first so-called sister, be so quick to claim you and provide you with a whole family history? What was she thinking?" I found this issue of conflicting memories perplexing, and even following Muna's story was confusing me.

"You have to understand," Muna explained. "Many children were abducted in the south at that time. There were lots of missing kids. Afterwards people were desperate to find their daughter or son."

I was again comparing in my mind the situation in south Sudan with the Jewish people after the Holocaust. Did they also sometimes find the wrong family? I wondered. But the Jewish people from their very beginning have been experts in genealogies, and not just oral but written records—so it was probably less likely.

I saw in Muna the tragedy of her whole nation. I was beginning to understand too, the reason her story was so confusing. The shock this little girl had suffered beginning at age six, had closed her mind to many memories and had covered all of her past in a dense cloud. The confusion was a symptom of her trauma.

"So what name do you want to be called now?" I asked.

"I call her Maria," Andrew responded.

"You don't want Muna anymore?" I found it hard to think of changing her name.

"I use both," she said, smiling her beautiful smile.

3. Yien

Grass-covered mud huts (tukols) and shacks in the city of
Juba in south Sudan (iStockphoto)

Our Culture is Good

On top of the Mount of Olives a pink streak over the Edom
Mountains in Jordan hinted that a new day was beginning. As
the muezzin's "Allah Akhbar" rang out in stereo from minarets
around the area, suddenly a different sound drowned out the early
morning call to prayer.

"Hallelujah! Praise the Lord!"

Fifty tall black men poured out of a bus, singing exuberantly
at the top of their voices. Several also drummed on darbukas, the
typical Middle Eastern "goblet drum" made of aluminum with a
sheepskin head. Tucking it under one arm, they thumped out a
powerful African beat. After a round of praise songs, they gathered
in a semicircle around the one white man in the group, closed their
eyes, and bowed their heads.

"Amen!" they proclaimed and began lining up for the obliga-
tory photos with the Dome of the Rock's golden cupola as background.

"Okay!" John, their leader, said. "Let's go! We're entering
Jerusalem now, down this narrow road to Gethsemane."

The ecstatic worship continued non-stop. Anyone in the neighborhood who had managed to sleep through the Allah Akhbar was certainly awake now. Anyway, it was already the late hour of 6:00 A.M.

After a pause at the Garden of Gethsemane with its famous church and ancient olive trees, the Sudanese group entered the Sheep Gate, one of the seven gates to Jerusalem's Old City. From there John, followed by the ever expanding assembly, strode down the Via Dolorosa. The fifty Sudanese who came on the bus all lived and worked in Eilat, but had encouraged their friends from Tel Aviv and Jerusalem to join them on this special Christmas day, until they grew to over a hundred people.

One of the Sudanese men in the group was Yien. From our first encounters in the Shelter Hostel, I was attracted to Yien's friendly smile and quiet confidence. I enjoyed watching how willingly he translated John's messages from English into Sudanese Arabic.

More than simply interpreting, however, Yien had a natural manner of assuming authority. When the dozens of Sudanese children attending the meetings started jumping around and yelling, Yien stepped up to quiet them. We knew we could turn to Yien not only because of his language abilities, but for his spiritual discernment.

Having joined himself to the fellowship in the Shelter Hostel not long after arriving in Eilat five months previously, he was thrilled when he heard about the Christmas excursion to Jerusalem. Now that the long awaited day had finally arrived, Yien said he felt as in a dream walking down the Via Dolorosa. Since becoming a Christian in 1988 in Sudan, he never imagined he would have the privilege to walk in the footsteps of Jesus his Lord.

Yien didn't consider it a sacrifice to sit on the bus all night during the five hour ride from Eilat to Jerusalem. He said he remembered Christmas in Sudan when they always went to church at midnight. That life seemed so long ago now, as if those memories belonged to a different person.

Now, tourists moved aside as the drumming and singing Sudanese men proceeded down Jerusalem's ancient cobblestone alleys. As windows and doors opened, shopkeepers peered out at the joyous group. John had arranged for his friend, Murray Dixon, to preach a special early morning Christmas service for the Sudanese in Christ Church, the oldest Protestant church in Jerusalem, near the Jaffa Gate.

The familiar Christmas message of the babe born in a manger in Bethlehem took on new meaning for Yien and the others as they sat so close to where all these events actually happened.

"For to us a child is born, to us a son is given.... And you are to give him the name Jesus, because He will save His people from their sins" (Isaiah 9:6, Matthew 1:21). The Sudanese listened and reflected how that Child left His heavenly dwelling, coming to earth out of love for them. Jesus understood what it meant to be a refugee, far from your family and home.

The next stop was Mount Zion. Here the men were fulfilling their own prophecy—Sudanese coming to Mt. Zion. "From a people tall and smooth-skinned ... whose land is divided by the rivers ... gifts will be brought to Mount Zion, the place of the Name of the Lord Almighty" (Isaiah 18:7).

Yien particularly seemed barely able to contain his excitement. A long winding road had brought Yien from his village in south Sudan to this spiritual peak in his life.

Earlier John had said to me, "Yien isn't Dinka like many of our Sudanese friends. He's from the Nuer tribe. It would be interesting to hear if his story varies from the others."

Although we could usually distinguish Darfurians from south Sudanese by their outward appearance, the distinction between Dinka and Nuer wasn't as clear to us. I invited Yien to our house for an interview. Prompted by my questions, he gladly spoke his story into my tape recorder.

*M*y name is Yien Chagor Reath from south Sudan. I was born in a large village called Nasir in Upper Nile State, a very good village in a perfect location next to the river.

Before the war in south Sudan we lived a peaceful, simple life. We were happy and had everything we needed or wanted—family, community, a rich land and our cows.

My father was a farmer and worked in his garden and fields. Neither he nor my mother went to school because during the English colonial period no one in our tribe attended school. So my parents just took care of us and raised grain and cattle. I grew up in a small house with my mother, three brothers and my sister.

My father married two wives but he died when I was young. So according to our tradition my uncle took responsibility for us and provided all our needs. Later on he went to north Sudan as a soldier. From then on my grandmother, a wonderful woman, cared for us.

I am from the Nuer tribe. What is special about the Nuer culture? We are one of the largest ethnic groups in southern Sudan and western Ethiopia. We are known as one of the very few African groups that successfully fended off colonial powers in the early 1900s. Our Nuer warriors were some of the most successful in all of East Africa. Although our numbers were smaller than the Dinka, in cattle raids against them we often came out victorious because we were so well organized.

Although to outsiders we may look similar, and we have some of the same customs as the Dinka, in fact we are a distinct tribe.

The Nuer society is based on democracy—all people are equal. No one can say to someone else, 'I'm better or higher than you.' We don't have leaders in the same way that other tribes do.

But respect for elders is important to us. We honor our parents and all older people. This is one of the Ten Commandments and it's also a rule with the Nuer. When I was a child I never could have imagined arguing with my mother or grandmother or not obeying them. I'm shocked when I see Israeli children who are disobedient to their parents. But also among us Sudanese refugees, since we are no longer living in our villages, we have lost many customs of our tribe. This makes me sad.

Hospitality is another important value to us. If you come into the land of the Nuer we will invite you to stay. Even if you don't want to return to your own country, you are allowed to live among us for as long as you like. We believe that a guest is sent by God and bestows a blessing on the host's house and family.

'Welcome. This is your house,' we say. 'You are our friend.'

And the Nuer elders instruct our children saying, 'You mustn't do anything to harm or bother our guests.'

You don't have to bring anything with you when you go to visit Nuer—we will provide all your needs and will give you our best food. It's like in the Bible when Abraham invited the three angels into his tent and ran to prepare food for them. Even though we Nuer didn't have the Bible in our own language, I believe that God writes the Ten Commandments on everyone's heart.

Cows, of course, are central to our culture as a sign of wealth, a source of food—milk and beef—and as a religious symbol. Now that many of us Nuer are Christians, we no longer worship our cows.

When a boy reached the age of sixteen or seventeen, he passed through a special ceremony to become a man. A group of ten or twelve boys was separated for six weeks and given select food and instructions on how to become a man.

A particular elder who is an expert takes a knife and makes cuts on your forehead.

'Sit very still!" he told us. 'You want the cuts to be straight like furrows in a field.'

I was 16 when it happened to me and I can say that it was very, very hard—so much blood! You can see the lines on my forehead. After this you are strong and can fight a lion or a tiger.

'You aren't boys anymore,' our elders explained. 'You've entered a new phase in your life. When we kill a cow you are able to eat meat set aside for men only.'

That's how it is with us Nuer. Certain parts of the cow are reserved for specific age groups and sexes. The chest part of the cow is set aside for young men with scars. Men older than fifty years can't eat that portion. The cow's back section is reserved for those older men. Our belief is that it's an honor to eat the part assigned to you, because it gives you standing in the community.

Our culture is good for us; however we cannot live like Nuer when we are outside of our country. But we still remember our heritage, respect elders, and will never say something bad to someone we don't know. That's how we were brought up.

We were surprised when we came to Egypt and found life was so different. Also in Israel the life is unlike the way we were educated in our villages in south Sudan. My childhood was very happy; but when the war began, everything changed and darkness fell over our beautiful land.

I grew up in Nasir until I was eleven years old. At that time my mother said to me, 'I want to take you to Malakal, to go to school there. You have an uncle you can stay with.'

Malakal was the big city in our area. I trusted my mother to know what was best for me. She wanted me to receive a good education.

So at that time, in 1992, I walked for three weeks with my mother and a group of twenty other people from Nasir to Malakal.

'Don't sit down,' my mother encouraged me when I was exhausted and thought I couldn't continue.

'Don't be afraid, God is with us,' she comforted me when I heard sounds from the bush on the dark nights.

On the way we prayed to God for protection from wild animals like lions and tigers, as well as from rebels who were also trying to kill us.

Due to the fighting between the SPLA and the government army at that time, the security was strict around Malakal. The soldiers stopped and questioned us individually and only after a day did we receive permission to enter. Even though the rain was pouring down, they just left us outside to suffer. The atmosphere was tense because if you gave the wrong answer they put you in jail and might kill you. But they didn't interview me, because I was just a boy.

I stayed in Malakal for one year attending primary school in the English and Arabic languages. Eventually I completed the primary as well as secondary schools and received a high enough mark on my matriculation exam to qualify for university.

I looked forward to continuing my education and studying economics and management in order to help my family and my country; but many things were against me.

Yien's life had taken a smoother and easier route than Gabriel's. True, he had spent years studying away from his immediate family, but at least he had a high school education and the hope to go to university.

What brought him to the extreme step of jumping across the barbed wire fence between Egypt and Israel in the middle of the night under the fire of bullets?

No One Will Know When We Kill You

One of the greatest longings of our Sudanese friends is for education. Those like Gabriel whose formal education was interrupted, and those like Yien who succeeded in graduating from high school desire to contribute towards building a new society in south Sudan.

They struggle in Israel because not only do they have no permanent status, but they aren't able to progress towards their goal. Gabriel would love to study agriculture and theology. Yien also wants to study theology. We are sad to see these intelligent, motivated men working as cleaners in hotels. I have no doubt that under other circumstances Gabriel and Yien would be leaders in their chosen fields, tribes and nation.

Although we've heard proposals to open a program to give selected men and women the opportunity to obtain higher education in Israel, many barriers stand in their way. Funding is a problem and so is language. Hebrew won't be an option for some time; and for many, their level of English isn't high enough to study.

Could the Israeli government, with contributions from

interested organizations, help them in return for a guarantee that
they would return to south Sudan to use the knowledge and skills
they acquire? Most of our friends would like to go home, but
who determines when the situation is safe enough?

*I*n Sudan there is a big difference between life in the city and
the village. Someone from a village will find it very difficult to live
in the city if they have no family there. I went to university for
six months in Khartoum but found it impossible to live on my own
in a rented apartment. I had no one to support me financially or
emotionally. I longed to go back to Nasir to see my mother since I
hadn't seen her for fifteen years, but transportation was a problem
in our area at that time, and I had no money.

Sudan's policy, like that of Israel, is for young people to serve
three years in the army after they finish high school.

Since everyone goes into the service, I thought I wanted to go
too. It would help my future. In 2002 I began my army training.
Unfortunately though, many soldiers were sent to the south to fight
the SPLA. When I found they wanted to send me there, I left the
army and went back to Renk to live with the uncle I'd lived with
during primary and high school.

I thought that maybe I could join the police. But in Sudan, if
you don't have connections with important people, you have no
chance to succeed. Everything has to do with who you know and
who your relatives are. Someone like me, a Nuer from a village in
the south, has no opportunity to be accepted.

When you come from a war-torn area and all your family is
scattered and you can't go back to your home, it's hard to find
your way in the world.

Since the army and police didn't work out, I decided I'd
study theology, thinking theological studies should bring me
closer to God. I considered myself a Christian, and I imagined
this would help myself and my family too. I thought my Sudanese
graduation certificate was sufficient to allow me to study in the
Protestant church in Khartoum. I heard that they paid all the

students' expenses. But I ran into the same problem—if you don't know any key person in the church, you won't be allowed in the seminary.

We who have strong networks of friends and family often take that for granted. Through our contacts with our Sudanese friends, I was learning that the hardships facing refugees encompass many more areas than I had ever imagined. Their lives are stunted physically, emotionally and mentally. They are adrift in the world with no anchor and no home port.

I heard that the Protestant church in Renk, a town north of Malakal and on the border of north Sudan, had a children's program and could use workers. I decided to join them. I could live there with my uncle and his family.

These were children who had parents and went to school in the morning. The church had organized enrichment programs for them in the afternoon and provided them with meals.

This is a little like what we do with the Sudanese children here in Eilat who come to the Shelter in the afternoon—we play games or football with them and have Bible studies.

We shared the love of Jesus with them. I really liked this work and for the first time felt that I was doing something positive. I was able to forget my own problems while I was helping the children.

But in Renk my problems with the Sudanese security began. The mujahideen, Islamist guerillas, had a lot of power in that area and violently opposed us. Like the Janjaweed in Darfur, they were supported by President Omar Hassan al-Bashir and his government soldiers.

One morning I was in the church library distributing breakfast to the children—bread, tea, chocolate and biscuits—when some mujahideen walked in. One of them pinned a notice on our bulletin board.

'Excuse me,' I said to them. 'This bulletin board is only for church information; not for general use.'

I naively thought I could reason with them, though of course I could tell they were mujahideen. You can easily recognize them by their dress. They look like the pictures of the Hamas terrorists you see on television. They have checkered scarves like the one Yassar Arafat wore tied around their heads and covering everything except their eyes. They don't want people to see their faces.

'Don't you know who we are?' they demanded. 'We're from the army and we can do as we want. You can't refuse us.'

'I'm sorry,' I continued. 'I'm not the one who made this rule. Our church leaders told me, "You mustn't allow anyone else to tack papers on our bulletin board."'

I was becoming more and more nervous as I saw the hatred in their eyes and heard the harshness in their voices, but I still couldn't have imagined what would happen to me the next day.

In the evening they returned. 'Tomorrow,' they said, 'you must leave this place.'

My home was not far from the church and I used to bicycle to and from work. The next day I was riding my bike down the road when a car driven by mujahideen stopped next to me. Someone grabbed me and threw me into the car. My hands were tied behind my back, my eyes covered, and I was driven to the security headquarters, where the blindfold was taken off my eyes.

I saw a person sitting in a chair opposite me. 'Do you know why you came here?' he asked.

What a crazy question, I thought. As if I voluntarily decided to come here to jail.

'I have no idea what I'm doing here or even where I am,' I answered. 'I was on my way home from work on my bicycle and

Gabriel, John and friend overlooking Jerusalem

Gabriel's father, born into a family of Dinka chiefs and raised in a village, went to school under English colonial rule and became a teacher

Grass-covered mud huts (tukols) and shacks in Juba, capital city of south Sudan
(iStockphoto)

Refugee huts in southern Sudan (iStockphoto)

Refugee camp in northern Sudan
(iStockphoto)

Child in a camp for internally displaced people, Darfur (iStockphoto)

The Egypt-Israel border that the refugees crossed

Above and below: Sudanese women and children outside refugee housing on Kibbutz Eilot in Eilat, Israel

Sudanese refugees joining in worship at a Friday night (Shabbat evening) meeting at the Shelter

A party with Sudanese dancing at Kibbutz Eilot

"Fun Day" outing with Sudanese children. (The author is front and right.)

Muna Maria and Andrew with their children

Sudanese boys in their Christmas suits at the Pex's home

John and Sudanese boys on Mt. Solomon near Eilat

John and Sudanese men and boys at Timna Park

Kids in the Shelter on Friday night

Football team

Above, below and facing page: Meeting in Eilat on Jan. 9, 2011—day of the referendum vote in Sudan when the south voted to be independent from the north

A successful vote could mean freedom for south Sudan and the possibility for the refugees of returning to their home

Muna of Darfur

some men caught me and forced me into their car.'

'Why didn't you allow our people to put our notice on the bulletin board at your church?' he asked.

'I told them at the time, my supervisor told me that no one from outside was allowed to post information.'

'We are the government security, and we are responsible for everything. If we kill you, no one can even ask about you.'

I kept silent. What could I say? I never imagined that my refusal to let them tack their paper on our bulletin board would lead to my arrest. But awful things were happening in south Sudan. People regularly were apprehended, tortured, and killed for no reason.

I spent three days all alone in a detention cell. The building was so flimsy that the rain and wind came through the ceiling and walls. The mosquitoes which swarm over south Sudan were my only companions, attracted by the water on the ground. With my bound hands it was torture to have the mosquitoes buzzing and biting me with no way to protect myself.

No one knows where I am. Even my family doesn't know. How long will they leave me here? I wondered.

My opportunity came on the third night. They untied my arms to allow me to sleep and neglected to close the door all the way. The rain began pouring down as if a cloud was emptying right on top of us, and my guard left his post. So I just fled, like an antelope pursued by a lion. I ran all night to a place far from Renk. I didn't dare go home—they might come back and capture me.

It was around midnight when I saw a driver headed north, struggling with his truck on the road. His clothes, drenched from the rain, stuck to him.

'Please,' I begged, 'can you take me with you?' He was surprised to see a man on that lonely road, but he must have sensed my desperation.

'Okay, sure,' he said. 'No problem.'

We drove six hours through the night and the next morning reached Rebek where my new friend let me off. From there I found a bus going north.

I approached the driver and said to him, 'Please, I have a problem. I need to get to Khartoum but don't have any money. My pockets are empty.'

I think he understood my situation. In those dreadful days people were used to helping each other.

After a four hour drive we reached Khartoum and I went straight to my uncle's house. I stayed with him for one week.

I spoke to my uncle. 'I had a problem with the security in Renk and that's why I left. But I don't want to stay in Khartoum.'

'So what do you want to do?' my uncle asked.

'Maybe you can find a way for me to leave Sudan. I can't live like this. I'm afraid I'll get killed if I stay here.'

Now I realize that I was far from God at that time and that added to my problems. But there in Khartoum I only knew that I was terribly unhappy and worried.

'I'm also in a difficult situation,' my uncle said. 'I'd like to help, but I don't have enough money to get you to another country.'

'Okay. I'll stay a little longer and see what happens.'

But I knew that the security forces from Renk might come to Khartoum to look for me. With them on my trail I couldn't go back to Renk to see my family. I was trapped.

'I'll try to raise the money,' my uncle said. 'I'll buy a ticket to Egypt for you.'

Prayer Requests and Answers

*I*n September 2003 my uncle obtained the money and handed me a ticket. I took the train from Khartoum to Wadi Halfa on the border with Egypt, and after that a boat down the Nile and through Lake Nasser. I arrived in Aswan, the first city in the south of Egypt, on October 4. From there I took a train to Cairo, a journey of a day and a half.

Thankfully I had a friend in Cairo, so I went straight to his house. Cairo is such a huge city that if you don't know someone, you are really lost. Even if you know someone you feel like one tiny mosquito in a huge swamp. No one knows you and no one notices if you live or die.

After a couple of days my friend said, 'Today I want to take you to the United Nations office to register. They'll give you a yellow card that's like having a visa. With that in your pocket, no one can send you back to Sudan. You'll be an official refugee. They'll also make an appointment for an interview for you. They'll ask you to tell your whole story and if they believe you are a genuine refugee, they'll change the yellow card to a blue one. With that you could be relocated to another country, like the United States, Canada or Australia.'

I was happy to receive that yellow UNHCR card, but they only scheduled an interview for me in April 2004. Six months!

What am I supposed to do until then? I thought.

I quickly found that life in Egypt was terrible. There's no work, and if by chance you do find work you earn about $50 a month. I was only able to eat because I stayed with my friend who receives money from his family in America. The days slowly dragged by while I waited.

When my time finally came for the interview they told me, 'Sorry. We don't have time now. We'll give you another appointment in four months.' I couldn't believe such lack of compassion and regard for the refugees' situation.

I was living with my friend in Ain Shams, ten kilometers from the center of Cairo. *I may as well find a church here*, I thought.

I had gone to church other times in my life, but lately I felt far from God. A human being is like this: When life is good, you forget God and think you can rule your own life—until the troubles begin. So I started going to church in Ain Shams. Interestingly, according to Egyptian legends, Joseph, Mary and Jesus stopped in Ain Shams after they had to flee from King Herod.

The Bible says that an angel of the Lord warned Joseph in a dream, to take the child and his mother and escape to Egypt. Joseph obeyed God. Herod, realizing he'd been outwitted by the wise men, killed all the baby boys in Bethlehem. Only after Herod died did another angel appear to Joseph in Egypt telling him to return to the land of Israel. So, like me, Jesus was also a refugee in Egypt.

I started going to the church often, to all the prayer meetings and Bible studies and became friends with the pastor of the church, David Dut. He is a Dinka who had lived in Nasir and also spoke Nuer, my language.

'Why don't you become part of our team and work with us?' he suggested after seeing I had become serious about my faith and was lending a hand.

My job was to organize the cleaning of the church, setting up the chairs, and preparing the list of speakers. I also helped to distribute aid to the refugees and other poor people in our area.

I lived in Egypt for two and a half years and found life there to be extremely difficult. It's hard to live when you are always in a state of uncertainty and you can't even support yourself but are dependent on others. I received 150 Egyptian pounds ($27) a month for my work at the church and a person can't live on that small amount.

All that time I was waiting for my interview with the UN. Every time they called me they would say, 'We have to reschedule your appointment for another time.'

In December 2005 the Sudanese Refugee Association organized a demonstration in front of the United Nations offices. We were protesting because they weren't helping us find permanent solutions to our problems, like resettlement to other countries. The Egyptian police began shooting at us, and our circumstances became even worse.

The official Egyptian news claimed that 33 people were killed, but we know that more died because many were wounded. In Cairo you made sure you didn't go to the hospital alone; someone had to go with you to care for you. If you went alone, they might kill you. They used to remove a person's heart or kidney or something else. So we know that those wounded in the demonstration who were taken to the hospital probably died there, with no choice but to be an organ donor.

Still, during my time in Cairo, I felt peace in my heart because I could live a simple life helping in the church. I thanked God for my life and His blessings. As long as I was alive I could receive more of His blessings.

In the beginning of 2006 I heard that Sudanese were crossing the border into Israel. I knew it was dangerous, but I believed this would be the best solution for me. The problem was that I had to pay the Bedouin smuggler 2000 Egyptian pounds ($360) and I had no savings at all.

'Jesus, I believe you want me to go to Israel,' I prayed. 'You know I don't have any money in my hand. But if it's your promise, I'll receive the money somehow.'

At that time I felt God close to me and began to share my plan and my need. I had some relatives in Cairo, and in all the time I'd lived there I hadn't asked them for anything. Now I decided to call them.

'I would like to go to Israel,' I told my relatives, 'but I don't have any money.'

'Okay,' one uncle said. 'If you want to go, I can help you with a little, maybe about $100. You can ask others to help also.' Slowly I received $500, enough for the trip.

'Thank you God,' I prayed. 'You answered my prayers, and I know You'll be with me all the way.'

I was so happy as I saw God fulfilling His promise to me. I thought about Moses leading God's people from slavery to freedom and about the prophecy in Isaiah 18 about Sudanese offering gifts on Mount Zion. Would this prophecy actually come to pass in my life?

After receiving enough money, I searched for the right person to take me to the border. In May 2006 I crossed into Israel with three other people. It was nearly midnight when the Bedouins dropped us off at the border. We were close enough to see the Israeli soldiers on the other side.

'Okay,' the Bedouin said. 'That's the fence. Just run!'

We had heard stories about Egyptian soldiers shooting people who tried to cross into Israel. The guys with me were all scared, but I didn't have fear in my heart.

'Friends,' I said to them, 'if we're afraid, we won't succeed. Let's be strong and we'll reach our goal.'

The Egyptian soldiers fired on us as we raced across, but when the Israeli soldiers noticed, they began shooting flares in the sky. It was as if the night turned into day and the Egyptian soldiers stopped shooting. But right before we actually entered, the Israeli soldiers stopped us.

'Why do you want to come here?' the officer asked. 'Please, you must go back.'

'You want us to go back?' I asked him.

'Yes,' he said.

'What do you have in your hand?' I asked.

'A gun,' he answered.

'Then please shoot us right now and let us die immediately,' I told him. 'That will be the same as if we go back to Egypt.'

He thought for a minute and said, 'Come.' But we still spent thirty minutes crawling over the tall barbed wire fence.

When we finally arrived, I had deep bloody scratches all over my body and my clothes were ripped to shreds.

'Thank you God,' I prayed aloud with my friends. 'You prepared the way and brought us over safely.'

'Wait here until a car comes for you,' the officer said. 'Don't be afraid. You are safe now.'

I am often asked why the Egyptian soldiers shoot the refugees as they are fleeing to Israel. After all, the Egyptians obviously don't like the Sudanese and don't want them in their land. One might think they'd be glad to have them leave. I've wondered about this and asked some of our friends.

No one really knows, but Sudanese have told me it's because the Egyptians don't like Israel either and most consider us their enemy, despite the fact that a peace treaty was signed between Israel and Egypt in Washington, D.C. in 1979. Officially a cease-fire is in effect and there is a degree of cooperation between the two countries; but in fact, Egyptian nationals are not free to visit Israel and their media is full of anti-Israel propaganda.

'The Egyptians don't want us going to Israel,' a Sudanese friend told me, 'because then we are joined to their enemy.'

*T*he army patrol car drove us to a base where they gave us water and food and a doctor treated our wounds. In the evening they took us to Ketziot Prison where I found many friends. Gabriel was also there during that time, but he arrived after me. I spent about twelve months locked up, including a time at Ramla Prison in the center of the country.

In prison we had lots of time to pray and read our Bibles. I came across the border with just the clothes on my back but I did manage to take my Bible.

We made a cross with pieces of wood we found and placed it high up on a wall. When the officer came by one day he asked the guards, 'What's this cross? Who allowed the Sudanese to put it up?'

So the guard came and told us, 'You have to take down the cross. Pray if you want, but without the cross.'

I was beginning to understand that Israel is a special country. Till then I didn't know what it meant to be Jewish—that they don't believe Jesus is the Messiah, even though it's written about Him in their own book. To me, Isaiah chapter 53 is clearly speaking about Jesus who paid the price for the sins of the whole world and who specifically came to the nation of Israel. 'We all, like sheep, have gone astray, each of us has turned to his own way; and the Lord has laid on him the iniquity of us all.... For the transgression of my people he was stricken' (verses 6 and 8).

I was used to Muslims being against Christians and killing us in Sudan, but now I saw that Jews were bothered when they saw a cross.

'God hears the prayers of our hearts. Outward symbols aren't important to Him. Let's move the cross to our house,' I suggested. 'The most important thing is that we continue to ask God to open the prison doors.'

Being in custody wasn't difficult; we were all together and encouraged one another. But what was hard was that we didn't know when we would be set free.

In May 2007 the Israeli government opened the door and we were all released from jail. I was sent to Eilat to work in a hotel and began to receive a salary. I found the work much better there than in Egypt. My monthly earnings in Eilat were enough to rent a room and to buy food and clothing. In Egypt I had worked ten to twelve hours a day, six days a week and my monthly salary had only been fifty dollars. This hadn't been enough to rent a room in a shared house. Now I had enough to send money to my family in Sudan, grateful to help them in that way at least.

People ask me, 'How is Israel different from Egypt?' I tell them that in Israel everyone is free to do what he wants. No one interferes in your life and when you work, you receive fair compensation.

But there's no place like home. Even if they give me everything I need, I'll still always miss my family.

Musings in Israel

From our first encounters, I recognized Yien's concern for his fellow Sudanese, his deep faith in God, and willingness to help, as well as his command of the English language. But I only understood what a deep thinker he was after having longer conversations and interviewing him. I appreciated hearing his thoughts about life and being able to gain a better understanding of the Sudanese mindset, at least from one man's perspective.

We refugees don't know anything about our future. We could go back to Sudan or we may stay in Israel, or move to other places. We try to follow the news, but are always hearing that the Israeli government doesn't want the Sudanese people. They may accept those from Darfur, but not from south Sudan.

But this doesn't make sense because al-Bashir, the president of the Sudanese government in Khartoum, accuses the SPLA in south Sudan of cooperating and receiving help from Israel. We in the south, not the Darfurians, are Israel's natural allies. The Arab nations send money to the Sudanese government to fight the SPLA, saying that Israel is helping the Christians in the south.

So why does the government of Israel treat us like enemies?

I was surprised when I came to Israel and found the Israeli people don't understand that we are their friends. Hearing us speaking Arabic, Israelis may think we are united with the Arab people and groups like Hamas and al-Qaeda. But it's actually the opposite. When south Sudan becomes independent, I'm sure we will have diplomatic relations with Israel. We speak Arabic because that's the language that united us in Sudan, but each of our mother tongues is our tribal language. For me it's Nuer.

I'm twenty-nine years old but am like a child without a future. The war destroyed my life, my family and my education. The war completely changed the course of my life. None of us Sudanese could have imagined we'd come to Israel, but I know it's God's plan. On our passports it is written: 'Good for all countries except for Israel.'

I was amazed to hear Yien speaking about his life as a refugee with no bitterness and with such acceptance. Clearly his faith has produced this positive attitude. Although he realizes that the Israeli government wants to send the refugees back to Sudan or Egypt, he's not stressed or worried about his future.

*M*y friends say that life is complicated in Israel. When we began working, problems arose every morning between the Sudanese and the Israelis.

'Please don't be surprised that we make mistakes,' I told our supervisors. 'Be patient with us. This is our first time working in hotels. We are from villages and aren't used to this life. For us it's confusing, like driving a car for the first time.'

We also encounter prejudice. People who believe in God know He made all of us in His image. But unbelievers discriminate and say, 'He's red or yellow or black or white.' Nevertheless, we don't give up and we continue to work hard to try to change our lives for the good.

Furthermore, we see many problems in the Sudanese families here because the life is so different. In Israel we found something called 'freedom,' especially for the women. Anyone can do what they want—a big contrast from south Sudan.

In Sudan when you marry you have to give your bride's family many cows. In Israel there are no cows. And both sides of the family have to meet and determine if the bride and groom are compatible. Most of us in Israel have either lost our families or don't know where they are. Many young men and women begin living together without getting married. Our whole family structure is broken down.

But in spite of all these challenges, you won't find a Sudanese who says, 'I hate Israel.' Maybe our life, work and families aren't what we expected before we came here. When we were back in Sudan we loved Israel. But even if the government of Israel sends us back to Sudan or to Egypt, we still wouldn't say anything bad about Israel. Because we know that God brought us here. He has a plan for each Sudanese person just as He has a plan for the whole world.

The problem is that many of the south Sudanese people are far away from God at this time. They aren't interested in fulfilling God's plan for them. I pray they will come back to God and worship the God of Israel on Mount Zion in Jerusalem.

When we were in jail, we all prayed. But many were just asking for God's benefits—to get out of jail. But when they were free, they forgot about God. They lied to God and said, 'Release me and I'll serve you.' But now they don't fulfill their vows.

We shouldn't believe in God for how we can profit—for a car, food or other material things. We should believe in God for who He is and because He loves us so much.

We have suffered too much and are still suffering. In our twenty one years of war, two million people have died. Some people look to the SPLA to take care of south Sudan, but I turn to God.

Epilog

*I*n 2009, I met a young woman from Switzerland staying in the Shelter. Jasmin came to Eilat to teach English to the Sudanese refugees. As I helped Jasmin translate weekly Bible studies, we got to know each other well and realized we had the same desire to serve the Lord. We shared with John and Judy and other friends about our growing relationship. At first they had reservations—mainly because of the great differences in our backgrounds as well as the possible obstacles having to do with my refugee status. We were aware of the challenges and met for counseling with another couple of friends.

Gradually, however, they were all convinced of our sincerity and love for one another. Four months after we met, the community celebrated our engagement with a big party in Kibbutz Eilot. Jasmin's parents even came from Switzerland to join us.

On May 22, 2010 we were married. The Lord opened the door for me to return to Sudan. A few weeks later Jasmin returned to London, her place of residence, and began the process of organizing a visa for me. After four months of separation and a lot of official correspondences, I miraculously received a visa for England.

We currently live and work in England but are hoping to return to Africa so that I can go to Bible College. For many years, I asked God to make a way for me to study theology in order to be better equipped to serve my people. I also asked God to allow me to cast my vote on January 9, 2011 regarding the referendum for an independent south Sudan. These prayers, as well as my request for a suitable wife and companion, have been wonderfully answered by my faithful Heavenly Father.

I am very thankful for all the help I received during my time in Eilat, especially from John and Judy. They treated me like a son, the way they loved me and invited me to all the Jewish feasts and even their son's wedding. I hope our paths will cross again one day and that they'll be able to visit my family in Sudan. I would love for my family to get to know the people that have done so much for the Sudanese in Israel.

The expression on Yien's face as I read these pages aloud made all my labors worthwhile. After taping his story, I listened and typed it on my computer. Then I began the complex task of editing Yien's words and thoughts into a readable text. To verify my accuracy and clarify questions, I read my version aloud to Yien and made corrections—the same procedure I followed with Gabriel, Muna Maria, Rose and Muna from Darfur, except that with the women, it was necessary to use an interpreter.

Yien was quiet as I read, mostly just nodding his head and smiling.

"I can't believe how you wrote my history," he said. "It's very, very nice. That's just what I tried to say, but you did it better."

4. Rose

Child in a camp for displaced
persons in Darfur (iStockphoto)

I Don't Understand War

Some of the most tragic incidents on the border are when
families become separated. When it is the mother that becomes
separated from her family, it is very taxing on little children
starved for attention and their busy, working father who is trying
to cope.

For months, we went daily to the village for hotel workers
at Kibbutz Eilot after we first made contact with the Sudanese
because we saw so much need there. It felt like we were in
an African village transported to a dilapidated holiday village in
Israel. Constructed on the edge of the kibbutz a few kilometers
outside Eilat, it was built as a low-budget guest house. The one-
and two-story buildings are grouped around a parking lot, dining
room, club house, and an open area that perhaps had once been
a garden. However, at this point, the dining room and club house
were closed, the parking lot rutted, and the garden area was

nothing more than brown sand with papers and empty soda bottles scattered on the ground.

Under a couple of spreading mango trees, whose fruit was plucked and eaten while still hard and green, groups of men and women sat separately on the ground. Children ran everywhere. Whenever we visited, we always saw little Ramzi on the hip of one of his sisters, Rauyia, age five, or Rimas, age seven. The sisters seemed too serious for their young ages.

We learned that their father, Shabbi, worked long hours in the hotel and their mother had been caught on the border and had been sent to an Egyptian prison. I noticed even on the coldest evenings, they frequently were wearing thin clothes and sandals. Their father left for work before they awoke and they dressed themselves. Each time I visited I tried to take one of them on my lap, to give them the mother cuddles they were missing. Rauyia and Rimas melted into my arms and often fell asleep.

One evening as I held a dozing Ramzi on my lap, I became aware of his soaked sweat pants and the smell of urine. I felt bad suggesting to Rauyia that she should change her brother's diaper once in a while. The sisters were obviously doing their best, but how could little girls be responsible for changing their brother's full diaper and wiping his dripping nose?

Months after observing the sad little threesome wandering together around the workers' village each time we were there, we finally received news that their mother had been released from the Egyptian prison and had successfully crossed into Israel. Regrettably, the Israelis then placed her in the Ketziot Prison for border infiltrators. After tons of patience and phone calls to the prison authorities by Yuval, the big-hearted manager of the village where the children lived with their father, the day finally arrived when Shabbi could go meet his wife in Tel Aviv. The three children, ages two, five and seven, stayed alone in their apartment that night.

I wondered how the children would react to their mother. Ramzi, age two, undoubtedly didn't remember her any more. He didn't know what a mother was.

Driving into the village the next day, I saw a beautiful woman wearing slacks and a colorful, stylish blouse, and holding Ramzi. I bit my lower lip as my eyes filled with tears. The girls stood shyly next to her, and for the first time I detected faint smiles on their faces. I was finally going to meet the woman we had been praying for.

The woman stepped forward and we kissed each other on both cheeks. "I'm Rose, Ramzi's mother," she said.

After that I made a point of seeking out Rose. She settled into life in Israel remarkably quickly. Always well dressed and with a warm smile on her face, Rose loved to come to the day care center for the Sudanese children and volunteer her time, a task mostly avoided by the other mothers.

We couldn't understand the problem, but the mothers seemed to have a hard time letting other people correct their children. When one woman, however mildly, tried to instruct a child not her own, a fight between the mothers was likely to break out. Thus, we admired Rose's bravery for venturing into the complex world of the day care center.

Several months after her arrival, Rose announced that she was pregnant. She continued to work in the hotel until the birth, as do most Israeli women.

Intrigued by her story, I found the opportunity to record Rose's words on a Saturday, her day off.

My name is Rose Biun. I was born in 1984 in Abiye town, which is located on the border between south and north Sudan. Abiye used to be a small, peaceful place to live, surrounded by green fields and forests. My father was a farmer like most of the other men. He had a small piece of land where he grew vegetables and raised goats and cows. I have two brothers and two sisters. They are all alive in Sudan.

How significant, I thought, that one of the facts a refugee would think important to include in her life's story is whether her family is alive or not.

Abiye is unfortunately often in the news from Sudan. Various tribes and ethnic groups inhabit Abiye, including the Dinka people predominant in the south. The disputed enclave is claimed by both the southern Sudanese government as well as the central government of northern Sudan.

Abiye is blessed, or cursed, to sit above a large oil field. This border town was one of the thorny side issues with the Comprehensive Peace Agreement in 2005, the official end to the war between the north and south. According to the terms of the agreement, the oil wealth was meant to be shared between both sides. Many southerners say, however, that the Sudanese government has fallen short of fulfilling its promises.

In the periodic border skirmishes, people are uprooted from their homes. Nevertheless, even when, in May 2007, fifty thousand people were forced to flee Abiye, life in southern Sudan was much quieter than in the years before the agreement.

In 1983, the year before I was born, the Second Civil War started. I don't understand everything about the Civil War in Sudan, but I know it ruined the lives of millions of our people—so many died or became refugees. The Sudanese government in Khartoum arrested my father and grandfather and killed many of my relatives.

I know that John Garang was good and that al-Bashir isn't good. He and his forces slaughtered innocent people, raped women, and burned villages—even in Abiye, my hometown.

My father eventually joined the army of John Garang and became a fighter with the SPLA. He wanted to defend his homeland. I saw him only once, because the government soldiers didn't allow him to enter Abiye.

I know my father is alive now and I know where he is, but I have no contact with him. After the peace agreement, my father went to Khartoum. I was able to speak to him when I was in Egypt.

But afterwards he went back to Abiye which has no phones.

I was the last of five children. My mother had problems during my birth, so afterwards she wasn't able to have more children. When I was eleven years old I began school in Abiye. I was excited to dress in my nice uniform and to join the other children going to school. When I was 13, I came home one day and saw my mother lying on her mat. I was used to seeing her always working.

'I don't feel well,' she said. She was curled up in a ball, holding her stomach, and scrunching up her face in pain. She had terrible diarrhea, but we had no doctors in our area.

I watched my mother becoming weaker and weaker and two days later she died in front of my eyes.

'Maybe it was cholera,' people told me later.

That's a terrible disease that kills quickly, and many people die from it in Africa.

After my mother died in 1997 I stopped going to school so that my brother—who was two years older than me—could study. I worked on our land, growing vegetables such as okra which I took to the market to sell.

When I was little we had one church in our town and we went there all the time. Today I hear there are many churches in Abiye. A long time ago my grandfather had no religion, like most people in our area, but then my grandmother and mother became Christians. In our family each person was free to choose his own religion. My uncle became a Muslim as well as my sister and big brother. But the other three of us children are Christians.

Why did we choose one religion over another? We chose what seemed better or more convenient. When I came here to live on the kibbutz, a friend told me about Jesus.

'If you say you're a Christian,' she told me, 'it's more than just choosing a religion. You have to understand what Jesus did for you. He loves you and died for your sins.'

She explained a lot to me because we used to work together in the day care center. When the children were sleeping we had time to talk. After all I'd been through, I knew God was watching over me and I wanted to understand more about Him.

But back to my childhood. I didn't continue working on the farm for long, after my mother died, because no one was responsible for me and my brother. My big brother had run away and though we searched for him, my mother didn't see him before she died. My oldest sister wasn't around at that time either. Later she married and went to Khartoum and now has six children. My other sister eventually finished school, went to university, and began working for the government.

With no one to care for us, life was difficult for my brother and me. The family gathered together to decide what to do with us.

'We want you to go to your uncle in al Ubayyid,' they told us.

That's a city in central Sudan, very far from our home.

My uncle was good to us, but the situation there was dangerous because the government security forces were arresting people for no reason. No one felt safe and we couldn't stay there.

'You'll have to go to your other uncle in Khartoum,' the first uncle told us. 'I'll help you to escape.'

In 2000 my brother and I moved in with this other uncle. He lived in the south of the city in a place called Jabel Awelia.

A veterinarian, our uncle was often without work as were many people in Khartoum. It wasn't a good life there. My uncle and aunt had a decent house, but they already had seven children of their own before we joined their family. We were often without food. I remember going to the market to look for leftover vegetables. Sometimes God sent someone to our house with food, exactly when we needed it.

One day I went to the shuk, the large outdoor market in Khartoum, to do the shopping for the family. Shabbi, who later became my husband, had a restaurant there. He offered Sudanese food like *ful*, one of our national dishes. We often eat *ful* for breakfast but it's tasty any time of the day. *Ful*, consisting of round brown beans, mashed and slow-cooked is served with olive oil, parsley, onion, garlic, and lemon juice.

I was young then and shy, so I avoided eye contact with the men in the market. But Shabbi started talking to me. Later he told me how he noticed me and decided he wanted to get to know me. I saw that he was nice looking and polite and seemed to like me.

'If you are interested,' I told him after we'd seen each other several times, 'you'll have to come home to my family and ask for my hand.'

That's how we do it in Sudan; marriages are arranged through the family.

'But I'm not sure they'll agree,' I said, 'because you aren't from our tribe.'

The fact that Shabbi was Muslim and I was a Christian wasn't a problem, but rather that we were from different tribes. My uncle wouldn't have minded if I'd married a Muslim because he was Muslim himself.

I was nervous the day that Shabbi came to meet my family. I already sensed what the outcome would be. All the family sat down together and Shabbi began.

'I would like to marry Rose,' he said. 'I love her and will care for her.'

'I don't believe you can provide enough cows for our family,' my uncle answered. 'We're a large family and we'll need at least forty cows from you.'

According to the Dinka tradition, the husband has to give cows to everyone in the family. All my relatives—uncles, aunts and cousins—had been sitting together already to discuss my possible marriage. Each was entitled to a portion of the dowry. Of course in cities the man couldn't really provide cows nor did the family need them, so he gave the equivalent in money. Many Sudanese families forced their daughters to marry a man who was old because he was rich and could distribute cows or money to all the family members.

Shabbi was a hard worker and managed his own restaurant, but because his father had died and he alone supported his mother and sisters, his family was poor.

'Any less than thirty five cows,' my uncle concluded, 'and there'll be no wedding.'

'If you don't agree that I marry Shabbi,' I insisted, 'I'll leave our family. We love each other and can't be separated.'

'Okay,' my uncle said, 'if you don't want to stay with us, leave.'

So Shabbi and I went to the courthouse and married. We had known each other for a year.

After that we lived with his family in their home. We didn't have much money or even our own house, but I was happy to be living with the husband of my own choosing and to be starting a new, independent life.

Circumstances, like growing up in a war zone and losing her mother to a deadly disease, had forced Rose to become independent at a young age. I could see how these events shaped her character and gave her the determination and ability to take risks that eventually brought her to Israel.

When the refugees began arriving in Eilat in May 2007, we went to hear a lecture by Yiftach Milo at the local college. He explained the background of the Sudanese Civil War, his experiences with working with refugees in Chad, and the latest information about their status in Israel.

"The refugees who arrive in Israel," Yiftach told us, "are the resourceful ones. They're not in the same category as those who pick up a few belongings and run across the border to Chad or Kenya or a neighboring country. To reach Israel requires planning and drive."

From Now on You'll Work for Us

The first years of our marriage were happy and peaceful. We married in the year 2000 and I soon became pregnant. Rauyia, our eldest daughter, was followed a year later by another girl, Rimas. My husband used to go to work in the morning and though we were poor, we usually had enough to eat. We lived like that until terrible security problems forced me to leave my home country.

My husband employed two workers from Darfur in his

restaurant. Because we had a large house they lived with us. At that time al-Bashir's government was fighting a war in Darfur, an area in western Sudan.

In the middle of one night, some security men came to our house, grabbed Shabbi and the two Darfurian men, and dragged them off to jail. I was terrified and couldn't imagine what they wanted from Shabbi, my wonderful husband.

'You're a spy!' they yelled at him. 'We know you have those men in your house in order to help the people of Darfur. You've been passing information and cooperating with our enemies.'

'I don't know what you are talking about,' Shabbi answered. 'I'm a simple man who sells *ful* in the shuk. You can ask anyone. I work hard to support my wife and my family. Those two men are my workers.'

'Tell us the truth,' the police demanded, 'or else we have ways of getting you to speak.'

Shabbi was lucky, though, because the police in Khartoum are often lazy. When they weren't paying attention, Shabbi and his two workers escaped, before they were tortured. Shabbi ran far away, over two hours from Khartoum. He didn't dare to come home.

I, of course, didn't know what had happened to Shabbi after his arrest. But a week later, the police came back to our home in the night and forced me to go with them. They took me away in their car, and then shoved me into a disgusting jail cell with my eyes covered and no food at all. Flies swirled leisurely in the still air and cockroaches scuttled across the floor. My nose burned from the overpowering smell of urine.

'What have I done?' I asked when I was allowed to speak.

'You know,' they answered. 'Where's Shabbi? He escaped and you know where he's hiding. If you tell us we'll release you, and if not—you'll be very sorry.'

'I do not know," I answered. 'I haven't seen him since the night you grabbed him. He never returned and I'm still waiting for him.'

Then they began beating me all over my body and screaming insults at me.

'Tell us about those men from Darfur who were working and

staying with you,' they demanded, 'or else we'll kill you!'

Finally after a week they understood that I indeed didn't know where Shabbi was, and they let me go.

They thrust a paper into my hands. 'Sign this,' they said. 'From now on you'll be working with us. If you have any useful information you must tell us. And you can't go any place without our permission.'

I had no choice but to sign, but from then on I began planning how I could escape Sudan. I knew my life was in danger. I didn't know where Shabbi was but I was concerned for my two little girls. I believed Shabbi would have communicated with me if possible, but he didn't want harm to come to us and many spies worked in Khartoum in those difficult days.

I went to the evangelist at our church in Jabel Awelia and asked for help. Before long he succeeded in obtaining a passport for me. I left Khartoum after having lived there four years and traveled to Atbara, a railway town. From there I took the train to Wadi Halfa on the border and a steamer boat to Egypt. I entered Egypt on March 11, 2004.

Thousands of Sudanese live in Egypt. I had an uncle from my father's side in Cairo with whom I could stay. Though his wife and I worked cleaning houses, we didn't even earn enough for food to eat. My uncle stayed home with the girls.

The Egyptians treated us horribly. They cursed us and barely paid us. I was constantly thinking and worrying about Shabbi.

In Cairo the only ones who cared for us were Christian churches. All of us refugees used to go to the Zamelek Church. They helped us see a doctor when we needed one, and distributed food. Before receiving their assistance we had to register and fill out a form. I found time one afternoon to sign up.

'Your name?' a kind man asked me.

'Rose Biun,' I answered and produced my documents.

'Your husband's name?'

'I don't have a husband. He was taken from us in Sudan.'

'Children?'

'Rauyia and Rimas.'

The girls and I all received identification numbers.

Unbeknown to me, five months later Shabbi also went to the church.

'Your name?' the same man asked him.

'Shabbi Aziz Tager,' he answered.

'Wife's name?'

'Rose. I haven't seen her and my two little girls since the security forces seized me from my home eight months ago.'

Shabbi noticed the man staring at his paper. 'Wait a minute,' the man said. 'Your wife and daughters already came to sign in. They're in Cairo!'

'How can I find them?' Shabbi asked in shock.

'They live in the town of Ain Shams, outside of Cairo,' he replied. 'Go to the church there and ask around.'

That's what Shabbi did. We Sudanese know how to find one another. Out of the blue, Shabbi stepped into our house one Friday afternoon.

'How are the girls?' he asked.

It was like the most normal meeting in the world, nothing really special, as if he had just come home from work for the day.

I was trying to understand the Sudanese. When Gabriel spoke about meeting his mother after fifteen years he spoke in a mono-tone—no excitement. Rose was separated from her husband for eight months and didn't know if he was alive or dead, and when they finally found one another, they acted as if it was just an ordinary day. Was this a way of protecting themselves from all their separations, losses and traumas?

As we came to know them better, we were discovering that the Sudanese family structure was different than ours. They even had a different way of describing their relationships. We came to realize that children, whom we thought were living with their parents, were actually calling the aunt or grandmother "mother."

"Why would your son live with his grandmother?" Racheli, our daughter, asked one mother.

"His grandma loves him and wanted him to be with her," she answered, as if it were the most logical thing in the world.

Now that we were living together as a family again, I moved out of my uncle's home and we rented our own place. But the rent was high—500 Egyptian pounds (about $90) per month. In Cairo a man had great difficulty finding a job and if he managed to work he only earned 200 pounds ($36) for the month. There were more jobs for women because we could clean homes. So I worked in the house of a well-to-do Egyptian family while Shabbi stayed home with Rauyia and Rimas. I earned 600 pounds (about $110) which left us with just 100 pounds ($18) for food and other expenses after our combined income—not nearly enough.

Sudanese men normally don't take any role in the care of little children. That is women's work and we live our lives quite apart from the men. How could Shabbi manage?

This reminded me of when our Sudanese friend Simon and his wife, Martha, came to visit us. Our daughter and son-in-law were here with their newborn baby, and Simon and Martha had come to congratulate them. Simon took the baby in his arms.

"In Sudan," he smiled, supporting the baby in one arm and resting the other around his wife shoulders, "we'd never be sitting like this. Men don't sit with the women, and when there, I never held a baby. But now I think it's good."

"Why can't you hold babies?" John asked.

"The baby might pee and then your pants would be wet," Simon answered, wiping the imaginary urine off his slacks. "A Sudanese man wouldn't like that."

In the beginning I worked from sun-up to sun-down and we barely managed. But when the landlord raised the rent, we became desperate. The woman I worked for told me that if I stayed with them full-time, not going home, she would pay me an additional

200 pounds a month. After that, sometimes I went for months without seeing my husband and girls.

The first apartment we rented had a telephone and we spoke once in a while, but after we moved, we didn't have a phone anymore and that made things more difficult. Once in a while Shabbi went to a pay phone and called the house where I worked so we could speak.

We had hoped we could both work to have enough to eat and to save money. But we couldn't leave the girls alone. In Egypt there are many bad people who knock on doors and when they find girls home alone—it's very dangerous.

The work was terrible and exhausting, and the money was still never enough. Somehow I kept going by reminding myself that at least we weren't on the street. We managed to pay the rent. If we had money we bought some food, and if not, we were hungry.

The Egyptians had no mercy. At 5:30 A.M. I woke up, drank a glass of tea, and prepared breakfast for the family. From then on I spent the whole day cleaning and working hard—washing floors, windows, dusting, and doing laundry. I had no rest at all.

After I served the family their midday meal, I washed the dishes and at 4 P.M. could finally eat myself—the leftover food. At 10 P.M. I had my evening meal and often didn't finish work till 3 A.M. And then I began again at 5:30. I usually didn't sleep more than three hours. But also in the night my mistress slept with a bell next to her bed.

In my sleep I'd hear that bell ringing and her calling out, 'Tea!' or 'Coffee!'

When I became pregnant with Ramzi I had no choice but to continue working. When I was six months pregnant I was forced to go with the family on vacation to Alexandria to take care of them and their friends. I was becoming weaker and weaker.

I found myself crying out to God, 'Why did you bring me to Egypt? If I leave my job we'll all be on the street, but how long can I continue like this?'

The Sudanese are survivors. Since first meeting them in Eilat, they have reminded me of the proverbial cat with seven lives. Or the cat that falls from a high place and always lands on its feet. Sudanese aren't easily defeated. Even after many setbacks or discouragements, they keep going and hope for the best.

Six weeks after Ramzi was born I returned to work. This time I found a morning-to-night job and I didn't have to sleep there. Shabbi now had three children to take care of, including a newborn baby.

I worked six days a week and had Sundays off, but in order to pay for the diapers and baby formula, I began cleaning another house on Sunday. That provided the extra money we needed. I nursed Ramzi at night after work and during the day Shabbi gave him bottles.

Ramzi ran into the house as we were hearing his mother's story. Rose laughed and said, "He doesn't look like he's lacking anything, does he?"

I agreed. "He's a big, strong boy."

He laughed a lot too—a radical difference from the woebegone, diaper-soaked little boy he was before his mother arrived.

I reached the point where I was so sick and weak I could barely drag myself to work. As I said, the Egyptians showed no compassion toward us. My boss didn't care about my situation, only about how much labor she could gain from me.

'You're too ill to work anymore,' she told me. 'Don't bother coming in tomorrow. I'll find someone else who can clean my house as it should be done.'

That's how my working career in Egypt ended. I went home to Shabbi and fell exhausted on the bed.

'What now?' we asked ourselves.

If I didn't work, we couldn't pay rent or buy food.

Sacrifice on the Border

John had asked Rose to tell her story into my tape recorder, but she obviously found it difficult to speak without prompting and without a clear idea of what was expected. Afterwards Joseph translated Rose's words from Arabic into English, but the result was bland, colorless and general.

Salaam, an Arab Christian friend of mine, offered to return with me to fill in the blanks. I told Salaam the questions I wanted to ask and she spoke to Rose in Arabic. An animated discussion between the two women followed. I could understand the direction of their talk and was delighted to see Rose remembering details and opening her heart—and to experience Salaam's involvement and concern. Periodically Salaam paused and translated Rose's words into Hebrew. I wrote it down in English.

"You and I are like psychologists," Salaam told me. "This really helps Rose, being able to talk about her life."

Rose, her face beaming, clearly appreciated our attention. And now we were reaching the point where I would learn what happened to her on the border—how she became separated from her husband and children.

In just two days we made a decision that changed our lives forever.

'I've heard many Sudanese are going to Israel,' Shabbi said.

We felt we had no other option open to us but to join them, even though I wasn't feeling well. We couldn't stay in Egypt, and no other country would accept us. But how could we afford to go? We had never been able to save any money in Egypt.

'I'll sell our television,' Shabbi said. 'And I have a friend in America who told me to call if I was ever in trouble. I guess now's the time.'

Shabbi sold the television for $100 and his friend sent him

another $100. But we knew that amount of money wasn't nearly enough for the five of us. The smugglers demanded several hundred dollars for each person.

'I'll just tell him the truth. What else can we do?' Shabbi said and went to meet the Egyptian who would connect us with our Bedouin guides.

Shabbi came home with good news. 'That man was kind,' he said. 'He agreed to take our whole family for just $200.'

We left Cairo in the morning and drove five hours through the desert in the Bedouin's truck.

'We're not far from the border now,' he finally announced. 'From here on we walk. I'll guide you to begin with, and then I'll point the way and you'll have to run.'

By this time we were joined by a number of other Sudanese whom we didn't know. We would be crossing the border as a group.

The night was very dark. We began walking a little and then stopped. We kept still while the Bedouin went ahead to scout around. We continued to proceed in the same way—stopping, scouting and moving slowly ahead.

'If I detect danger, we'll go back,' our guide whispered.

I felt myself becoming weaker and more tired as the night wore on. I could barely lift my feet at this point.

The Bedouin stopped and pointed. 'That's it there. Now you have to make a run for it. Don't stop until you reach the other side. There you'll be safe.'

As each of us adjusted his clothes and shoes and gazed into the blackness, I sat on the ground. I felt as heavy as one of the thousands of rocks surrounding us. At that moment we heard shots not far away. At whom or what were they shooting? Another group of refugees? Or maybe they had spotted us?

'Shabbi,' I said. 'I can't go on. There's no way I can run. I'm sick and weak. Let me die here. Better me than our children. If I come with you I'll endanger you all. Rauyia is big enough to run by herself. Let someone carry Rimas and you take little Ramzi.'

Shabbi didn't argue with me. He had no time. The group was ready to run towards the fence. He knew me and understood. I lay on the hard, cold ground and waited for the Egyptian soldiers to catch me.

'Don't let them shoot me,' I prayed. 'May the family make it to safety. And may we find each other again.'

Rose paused. We all needed a break.

"You'll have a lot to tell your children," I told her. "Maybe we can translate this story back into Arabic for them and they'll be able to read about their mother."

"I don't want to tell my children," Rose said.

She explained that when she was in jail, and Rauyia had to take care of little Ramzi, she had such a hard time—carrying her little brother around on her hip the whole day, changing his diapers, and feeding him. She used to cry to her father, "Where's Mommy? Why doesn't she come?"

At first Shabbi didn't want to tell her, but he felt he owed her an explanation.

"Mommy's in jail. She wants to be with us all, but the Egyptians won't let her out," he said.

Then Rauyia really began to howl, "Mommy's in jail!"

Shabbi was sorry he had told her.

Because there were many Sudanese trying to get into Israel that night, we were divided into groups, and I wasn't alone. When I sat down, four men, three women and seven children caught up with me.

When Shabbi's group crossed the fence, the Egyptian soldiers sensed people passing over so they moved in and began shooting. That's when they noticed our group. Apparently they didn't aim to kill but just to scare, so that someone trying to flee would be afraid and sit down.

We all froze, knowing that if we moved, they could kill

us. As we huddled on the ground, the soldiers loomed over and began cursing us. 'Why do you want to go to Israel? Don't you know there's no work there? Only prostitution! You're going into prostitution!' they screamed.

'Do you have passports?' their officer demanded.

'Yes, we have.'

'So take them out and give them to us.'

We each produced our documents from where they were hidden under our clothes and the Egyptians began reading them one by one. An army truck drove up; they piled us in and brought our entire group to jail.

Breakfast, Lunch & Dinner: Ful, Ful, Ful

I was alive but terribly weak. *Where are Shabbi, Rauyia, Rimas and Ramzi?* I wondered. *Are they alive? How will they manage without me?*

The Egyptian soldiers put us in a truck and took us to Rafiah where we stayed two days. Then we were moved to the jail in el Arish, North Sinai's capital city.

They locked up our group—the four men, three women and seven children—in that dirty jail with nothing to eat and nothing to do. The children were crying all the time. After two weeks an official came to us.

Actually he didn't come to visit us but because he heard that a group of Sudanese had been caught and a woman had been killed, he came to take the body. But when he arrived, he saw the hungry and crying kids.

'Okay,' he said. 'Here's 200 pounds ($36). Use it to buy food for the children.'

After that they began distributing money every day for us to buy food and diapers for the young children. But we adults still didn't eat.

For three weeks they took us once a week to the courthouse in Ismailia, a four hour drive.

They gave us food like bread, halva and cheese, but it was all rotten. When we tried to eat it we had diarrhea, because it was so unhealthy. So we didn't eat until our fourth court hearing. At that time, my cousin heard about my situation and came to me with money that allowed me to buy supplies for myself and the rest of us. For our food we used to give money to a prison guard and he went out and bought us what we needed. Actually all we ate was *ful* and some eggplant. Because near the jail was a small restaurant that sold only *ful*, morning, afternoon and evening we just ate *ful*.

When we stood in front of the judge the fourth time, my heart was beating hard as he looked down at his paper. *Maybe now I will finally be set free*, I thought.

'All those with children or who are pregnant are released from jail,' the judge declared. 'You will come with us to the passport office and those with passports will be returned to Sudan.'

I immediately understood—everyone else in my group was together with their family. Only I was alone—my children were in Israel with Shabbi, I hoped.

So I was returned to jail, without money.

My aunt, knowing I was in jail, asked permission to visit me. After filling out many forms she finally received clearance and brought me clothes, underwear, hair oil and money. In the meantime new women who had been caught on the border were moved into my cell. Then there were ten of us women in a small room the size of a bathroom.

We slept standing or sitting. And daily they brought in new women and weekly took them to court. I couldn't understand what was going on. Some women received a sentence of one year and were taken to the main prison. But I remained in jail in el Arish.

I used the money my aunt gave me to feed all the women. A pound was enough for twenty pitas and the *ful* cost 1.5 pounds. The jailer used to ask for extra and he kept the change for himself.

During all that time it was just *ful, ful, ful*. Sometimes it had sausage with a bit of peppers and spices in it. Everything else was expensive because the guard would have to travel and pay for a taxi. So we said that *ful* was okay. We had to eat something.

Only once I ate something different. An Egyptian woman was in the cell with me for two days. We became friends and she saw that all I ate was *ful.*

'When I get out I'll bring you some food,' she said. 'My house is nearby. What would you like to eat?'

'M'luchiya,' I answered. 'That's all I feel like eating.'

"Do you know what m'luchiya is?" Salaam, our interpreter, asked me.

I didn't know so I asked some of the Sudanese boys who were visiting us. "What's m'luchiya?"

They laughed as if surprised at my question.

They pointed to one of my house plants. "It's like that, with green leaves. You chop, mash and cook it. You can use olive oil."

"It's tasty?" I asked.

"Yeah," they answered with big smiles.

Rose continued her story.

So when that Egyptian woman was released she prepared m'luchiya, rice and grilled chicken and brought it to me. I was so happy that day. I shared it with the other women and we all ate that for two days, then went back to eating *ful*.

Nearly all of us there were Christians so we used to pray together and our faith strengthened us.

All the women came and went and I alone stayed in jail. I became famous and all the guards liked me and treated me well. Sometimes the women would fight among themselves. When they came in they might hide a razor blade in their mouth and the police wouldn't discover it during the usual examination. So they could hurt the other women.

But the guards would tell all the new women, 'This is Rose. No one will harm her because she's one of us.'

'Why do I have to stay here?' I asked the guards. 'Why can't I go to the big prison like everyone else? I could have more people to talk to, work to do, and could move around.'

'You don't want to be there,' they told me. 'There's just a lot of fighting.'

'Let me go and fight,' I said. 'At least I'll have something to do.'

'No, you'll stay here,' they said.

It was so terribly hot in jail because I was there during the summer months, from May through October. We had a small window in our cell but it didn't provide any ventilation. We used to throw water over ourselves to cool off, but even the water was burning hot since it came out of pipes exposed to the sun.

My aunt finally made contact with a lawyer who of course asked for money to release me.

'We will only pay you when Rose is free,' my aunt told him. 'But don't worry, you can trust us.'

'Okay, when she's released you will pay me 2000 pounds ($360),' the lawyer told my aunt.

That was a lot of money for my aunt, but she called relatives in Australia and they sent her the money.

My lawyer discovered that I had Ramzi's birth certificate.

'I can prove now that you're a mother,' he explained. 'Give me that document and they'll be required to release you according to the law.' But unfortunately by the time he organized everything it was nearly time for me to be freed anyway.

While we interviewed her, Rose's new baby, Rami, had been sleeping in their double bed. He began whimpering and moving around. Rose picked him up and put him to her breast to nurse.

"How old is he?" I asked.

"Two months," Rose answered.

A cute, healthy little boy born in Israel, I thought.

A week after that Egyptian woman brought me the m'luchiya, a guard came to my cell.

'Come, let's go!' he said and handcuffed me.

He put me in the police car and took me to another station where I was questioned again.

'Why did you want to go to Israel?' an officer demanded. I recognized him as the official in charge of national security. He spoke in such a threatening way.

I couldn't lie. I was a Christian and felt I must tell the truth.

'I wanted to go to Israel, and still want to, because I want to live and take care of my children,' I answered.

'There's no work or money there,' he said.

'I just want to live and take care of my children,' I repeated.

'Where are your children?' he asked.

'I don't know where they are. Do you think it's right to keep me here six months without any knowledge of my children? I want to find them.'

Of course I knew that Shabbi had attempted to cross into Israel with our three children, but I hadn't had any contact with them from prison. And at the time my aunt came to visit me, she also wasn't able to give me any details concerning my family's location. I was also trying to play dumb as much as possible.

'If you go to Israel, they'll make problems for you there,' he told me.

'I can't live here in Egypt—there's no way for me to support my family. That's all I want,' I said.

'In Israel there's no work, just prostitution,' the officer said. 'You and your husband will be prostitutes.'

'I don't care,' I answered. 'I'll work at anything where I can earn money. Even prostitution.' I was feeling desperate and just wanted to get away from that investigation and away from Egypt.

'Shut up!' the policeman shouted.

When they later returned me to el Arish, I still didn't know what would happen to me. That was on a Saturday, and on Sunday I heard a knock on my cell door.

'Gather your belongings and come with us,' the guard told me.

'Where to?' I asked.

'Cairo.'

I knew if they brought me to Cairo I would be going to the passport office. That was something positive—finally leaving the jail in el Arish.

'Why do you want to go to Israel?' the official in the passport office asked.

I was getting tired of always being asked the same questions.

'To live and to work,' I answered again.

'Do you have an identity card?' he asked.

I produced it and he called the police in el Arish, who told them my story—that I had been in jail there for six months.

'Okay, you can go to your family,' the official announced.

What can I do? I wondered. *I don't have any money. I have nothing.*

But when I stepped out of the building I met a Sudanese man on the street and asked if he could lend me a little money to call my aunt. He agreed.

'Take a taxi to our house,' my aunt said, 'and I'll pay the taxi when you arrive.'

My aunt couldn't believe I was standing in front of her. She had no hope I'd ever get out of jail. She had helped me a lot while I was imprisoned and knew all about my situation there.

I stayed with her for about a month. During that time I acted as if I planned on staying in Egypt. I didn't want the police officers in Cairo to think I would be trying to cross to Israel again. I even went and took out an Egyptian identity card. I was aware that I was being watched carefully by the Egyptian secret police. My luck was that the security forces in Egypt weren't efficient and the different branches weren't in contact with each other. Although I had told the national security officer who examined me while I was in jail that I wanted to go to Israel, I knew that the police in Cairo still wouldn't allow me to leave.

Shabbi had sent $500 to my aunt. He was in touch with her so he knew what was happening with me.

'I'm afraid,' I told Shabbi on the phone.

'Don't worry,' he reassured me. 'If you're too afraid you won't be able to do anything. I have a friend who plans to bring

his wife to Israel. You can go with them. He lives in Tel Aviv
and knows a good way to do it. It's important to get the right
people to drive you because of all the roadblocks and border police
in Egypt on the way.'

So after a month I told my aunt, 'I can't stay here any longer.
I have to try again.'

I knew that I would be doubly checked when they found out
I had already tried to cross once and had been caught and had
spent six months in jail. The police searched every car, looking
for Sudanese.

I, along with several other Sudanese, was hidden in a truck
that was transporting sand. We had to lie down in the back and
cover ourselves with the sand. Only our heads stuck out.

'When we come to a checkpoint,' the Bedouin smugglers told
us, 'you have to hide completely under the sand until we give
you a sign to come out. They won't suspect that a sand truck
has people in it.'

We traveled like that for three hours, checkpoint after police
checkpoint. Sometimes I thought I would suffocate.

Finally we passed through the final roadblock and could free
ourselves from that sand. A short distance further on, another car
waited to drive us into the desert.

They took us to a Bedouin camp and told us we would stay
there until they found a good time for us to cross. But after two
days I couldn't remain any longer. I felt I had to be moving or else
I would go crazy sitting there.

So I joined a group of four men who were also ready to move.
Carefully and soundlessly we advanced to the border. When I saw
the high fence, I didn't know I would have to climb over it. The
men had no problem but for a woman it was almost impossible. I
got stuck in the middle of the border with one leg caught in the
barbed wire and the other leg in the air.

The men had already jumped down the other side and were
running away because the Egyptian soldiers had begun shooting
when they noticed us.

"They left you alone?" I asked through the interpreter.

"Yes, they were as far away as the distance from here to the kindergarten over there."

Rose pointed across the grass to a low building one hundred meters away, a little longer than the length of a football field.

*D*esperate, I started screaming. 'Help! Please! Get me down from here!' I knew if the Egyptians caught me a second time I would be in big trouble.

One of the men came back, untangled me from my snare, and lifted me out. If he hadn't helped me I would probably still be in prison, or worse. I began running with all the strength I had and after fifteen minutes met some Israeli soldiers. They questioned us and took us to Ketziot Prison.

I was there in prison for three months. The situation was okay because we had three decent meals a day—morning, afternoon and evening. We slept in tents but could move around freely in the prison compound. The police treated us well, though they often questioned us.

'Do you know anyone in Israel?' they asked me.

'Of course,' I answered, 'my husband and three children.' I told them the whole story of my first attempt to cross, my capture and time in the Egyptian prison.

'Do you know where he is?'

Shabbi and I had been communicating through my aunt, so that's how we kept in touch and knew each other's whereabouts.

'He's in Eilat, working at a hotel in Kibbutz Eilot.'

Shabbi was doing everything he could to get me released. Yuval, the woman from the kibbutz who was the coordinator for the Sudanese, helped a lot and made many phone calls to the right offices and people. I knew I would get out eventually and I just had to be patient.

Finally the day arrived when Shabbi and Yuval came to meet me and take me to Eilat, to my children.

I knew that when I was away no one took care of my children. They cried a lot and were teased by other children. My daughters had no mother to braid their hair, so Shabbi kept it short and they were ashamed. They suffered so much.

Rauyia and Rimas had looked so mournful without their mother. And their short, boy haircuts added to their pathetic appearance.

"They're embarrassed," our daughter Moriah told me. She lived on the kibbutz near the Sudanese families.

All the other Sudanese girls had nicely braided hair. When, for a party, one of the other Sudanese women braided the two sisters' hair with extensions, they looked beautiful.

I arrived in Israel at the end of November 2007 and was in the kibbutz in February 2008. I couldn't believe I was finally there. I couldn't believe I was seeing my children again. When I had last seen Ramzi he was a baby, less than a year old. Now he was standing in front of me as a little man.

Epilog

Our daughter Moriah was working in a day care center on the kibbutz. The Sudanese who lived there were employed in one of the Eilat hotel chains, and the management decided to set up a day care center to enable the mothers to also work. Moriah, together with Salaam, my translator, cared for about fifteen cute children from ages eighteen months to four years. Salaam could speak to the little children and especially to their mothers in Arabic, but the language of the playroom was Hebrew and the children were learning quickly.

In August 2008 Moriah called to tell us that Yuval, her supervisor, had just brought a three-year-old girl with no family to her day care center. We drove over immediately and saw a beautiful little girl, dark skinned like a Dinka, wearing a pink shirt and yellow hospital pants. She sat on Salaam's lap. Her hair was braided in an elaborate pattern with red hair extensions, obviously done recently.

She was probably dressed up for the occasion of crossing the border, I thought.

"As far as we can understand," Moriah explained, "she was crossing the border with her mother and some other Sudanese. They walked a long distance after the Bedouins dropped them off and they grew tired and dehydrated and lost. The Egyptian soldiers noticed them and began shooting. The mother either dropped her little girl or handed her to a man who was part of the group. The mother was either killed or captured and the man made it across into Israel.

"They probably entered not far from Eilat; the man and the little girl were taken to the Eilat hospital. Both were dehydrated and received treatment. The man, who had no connection with the mother, believed that the girl's father was in Israel.

"The hospital contacted Yuval, and now here she is," said Moriah. "We don't even know her name. Yuval asked if Tom and I would take her home until they find her family. Tom is so excited he already called Racheli to say she'd become an aunt and he's looking for a child's seat to put on the back of his bicycle."

When we went to Moriah's home at the end of the day, the little girl was sitting on her lap crying.

"Now we know her name is Ashola," Moriah said. "We called in Rose who spoke Dinka with her. She played a bit with the other children and then fell asleep. I've asked some of the mothers to bring clothes for her. But now she just cries and won't even let me wipe her nose."

Just then Rose walked in with Shabbi and Ramzi. She lifted Ashola onto her lap and softly murmured comforting words to her and wiped her nose.

"I'll take her home," Rose said.

Looking at Shabbi she said, "Here's your baba."

When we drove out of the kibbutz an hour later we saw Rauyia and Rimas holding Ashola's hands with Rose and Ramzi nearby—a happy family.

"I just hope they find her mother," I said to John, "and that she's alive. The Sudanese have an amazing way of finding each other, so there's a chance they will find her."

When I saw little Shushu (that's what we call her) for the first time and heard she had lost her mother crossing the border, I immediately wanted to take her into our family. I thought about Ramzi being separated from me with no one to care for him. I felt somehow I would be turning the clock back and taking care of Ramzi.

We took Shushu to thank God for what He did for us, bringing us all together in Israel. I was so happy that I wanted to share my happiness with this sad, weak little girl.

But I must say that Shushu wasn't easy in the beginning. She found it difficult to fit into a new family with a new father and mother. She felt she had been taken from her real family and looked at us as the ones who were responsible for her pain. She didn't want to obey me and was very stubborn. That was a difficult period for us.

'Where's my mother, my brother and sister? Why did you steal me from them?' Shushu accused us.

But by the end she listened to us and began behaving much better.

Through our networking we succeeded in locating Shushu's mother and found she was in prison in Egypt. Yuval contacted the Red Cross and even Aliza Olmert, the wife of Israel's prime minister. We had patience, and finally after six months, we received news that Shushu could cross the border and meet her grandmother on the other side.

Shushu was happy to be going home again. She really understood.

'Don't worry,' she told me. 'I'll come to visit you.'

We bought new clothes for her and braided her hair. We sent her back with a whole suitcase of clothes.

About two months after I had joined my family in Israel, I found out I was pregnant. At first I wasn't happy with this news. I was trying to begin a new life with them and I knew that another child would be difficult for us. I had a job cleaning the house of a very nice woman. And I became very sick and lost a lot of weight.

'Why did you do this to me?' I asked God.

And I was already busy with four children when Shushu came to live with us. *Isn't that enough?* I thought.

But God gave us a gift with little Rami. The girls love him and so does Ramzi. Shushu has gone and now we still have four children. We don't want any more.

I had experienced many tragedies but now I thanked God that I had arrived safely in Kibbutz Eilot and was reunited with my husband and children. I don't know what the future will bring. But I trust God.

5. MUNA FROM DARFUR

Muna in Eilat

Sunny Days in Darfur

Am I prepared to hear Muna's story? I asked myself on my way to her house. *How will I react when talking to someone who fled from genocide?*

Whenever I saw Mohammed, Muna's teenage son, in the kibbutz village for hotel workers, he looked sad and distant.

"I understand they have a horrific story," John told me.

It was Tom, our son-in-law, who connected me with Muna. While working as a gardener on the kibbutz, Tom used to eat lunch in the communal dining room. One day he had sat at the table with Muna, and in her broken Hebrew mixed with Arabic she began telling Tom about her life. Too soon they both had to return to work, but Muna said she'd like to meet Tom again and speak more.

"Moriah asked her over tomorrow evening and we thought you might want to come too," Tom suggested to me. "I know you're collecting stories from the Sudanese."

Recording Muna's testimony would be complicated because she didn't speak English and I would need an interpreter. I had no idea who to ask.

Our daughter Moriah worked in the day care center for Sudanese children, knew many of the women, and understood their mentality. She felt Muna would be shy or sensitive about speaking in front of other Sudanese. So Moriah decided to invite just Muna and Mohammed. Having attended an Israeli school for a year, Mohammed spoke adequate Hebrew. That, however, also didn't seem right to us—a son translating such a painful subject for his mother.

"Why would she want to speak with you?" our other daughter Racheli asked when I told her about my plan. She wasn't the only one who had that question.

"Everyone likes talking about themselves and telling their story," I answered. I thought about when people ask me how I came to live in Israel or started to believe in Jesus, and I'm happy to share with them. Most people are flattered when others are interested in hearing their life story. And I thought it might be good for Muna to talk about it.

On the other hand, Muna's life was radically different from mine. I tried to put myself in her place. I hoped having someone to listen would bring her release and comfort, that the sharing of her burden would lighten it. I hoped she could understand my purpose—to let the world know of her own and her nation's dreadful suffering.

Moriah, Tom and I were sitting in their cozy living room when Muna and Mohammed (or Tom as he likes to be called now) came to the door. Muna, a wide smile on her round, friendly face and with skin the color of cafe latte, kissed Moriah and I on each cheek. She stands out from most of the Sudanese in Eilat whose color is more like Turkish coffee.

Muna was wearing a tight purple tunic over white pants and had a colorful scarf tied around her pony tail. The head covering distinguished her as a Muslim, like all Darfurians. Naturally I'd heard about the current genocide in Darfur, but with the majority of Sudanese refugees in Israel being Christians from south Sudan, I didn't know much yet about Darfur.

Since the Sudanese had started arriving in Eilat, I had begun reading books written about the "Lost Boys" who resettled in America in an effort to understand the Sudanese mentality and culture. Now I made a mental note to look for books about Darfur.

Moriah and I smiled a lot and asked about Muna's work and Mohammed's school. Moriah served tea and fruit; we wanted Muna to feel comfortable and welcome.

"I'm writing a book about the Sudanese in Israel," I explained. *Has Muna ever read a book?* I wondered.

"I want people here in Israel and other places too, to know what you've been through and what your life is like now."

Did this concept even make sense to Muna? I reached into my purse for my small tape recorder, hoping Mohammed might translate his mother's words. They looked at each other and Mohammed sort of shrugged his shoulders. I realized that neither of them was at ease with this arrangement.

So Muna stood up, walked to the other side of the room, and sitting in Moriah's rocking chair, she held the tape recorder in her two hands and simply began speaking in Arabic.

We sat silently and listened. Understanding little except the occasional place name, we were nevertheless moved as Muna poured out her tale. After about twenty minutes she collapsed in the chair, huddled over, and began crying. Moriah and I moved to sit on the floor at Muna's feet. We hugged her and prayed with her.

"Todah, chukran (thank you)," Muna said, trying to smile again.

After recording Muna's story, I prayed about who would translate and transcribe it onto paper.

"I'll ask Joseph," John said. "He recently came over the border and stays now in the Shelter. He speaks excellent English and isn't working yet. And besides, he's a kind man who I can already see wants to help the other Sudanese."

Two days later Joseph handed me eight neatly handwritten pages on stationary from the UNHCR, the United Nations High Commission for Refugees, where he had worked as an interpreter and interviewer in Cairo.

In tears I read and typed Muna's words onto my laptop.

I am Muna Ali Ismail from Darfur in Western Sudan. I was born on October 29, 1969.

My father was very well off and respected. He had cattle, which is important in Darfur, and money. There were five girls in our family. I never knew my father though, because he died when I was seven months old.

My uncle then married my mother in order to take my father's wealth and to have a son to carry on the family name after the five daughters. That was the custom in our tribe. Our uncle took us to live in Singi in East Sudan, which is around Muzzein in the Blue Nile State. He continued to care for me and my sisters. I went to school until the third grade.

When I was fourteen years old, in 1984, my uncle married me to his son, my cousin, Hassan Omar Suliman. For my dowry, since I was living as his daughter and marrying his son, my uncle sold cattle and bought a house and gold with the money. For us it was normal to marry at such a young age because most of my friends and family did the same. I didn't question my uncle's choice.

When I married we sold our house in Singi. We used the money to buy a house in Darfur, in Zalingei town where my husband was born.

Hassan Omar was a good husband and father. Those were happy years for me. We had no financial problems. My husband worked in Saudi Arabia before we were married, having gone there when he was eighteen years old. When he was twenty six he came back to marry me. He took all the money he'd earned and started a business as a cattle seller.

Muna made a sign with her hand, bringing her closed fingers to her lips and kissing them. I loved her animated use of body language and facial expressions.

My husband truly loved me and took care of everything. The sun was shining on us during those years. Sudan was good then. Our life was peaceful and quiet. We visited a lot with our extended family and had much joy as we celebrated weddings and feasts. I didn't have any worries except the normal ones for a mother with young children.

We had six children. I was fifteen when I gave birth to my twin sons, Hamed and Omar. I had such a big belly!

Muna leaned back in her chair, stretched her arms straight out, and traced the shape of that enormous, protruding belly.

My babies were born by caesarian section in the hospital because I was young and the babies were large. The twins were followed by Mohammed, Salah, Shamsidin and Charfedin—all boys. The youngest was very small, but the older ones went to school and were good students. I loved taking care of them, cooking tasty meals, and dressing them in nice clothes. Every year my children passed their school examinations.

We had a very good life because my husband was a successful cattle dealer in markets all over western Sudan. He was a prosperous trader, and we had a large, comfortable house with many rooms. Many fruit trees grew in our big garden. Nearby we had pens for our horses, cows, sheep and camels.

My husband employed three people to take our cattle to the market and sell them. They drove our three cars and brought the money they earned to our house and to the bank.

It's hard for me to think about those happy days. Today I can't sleep. I don't remember when I last slept well. I never imagined at that time that everything would suddenly change in such a horrible way. Darkness fell on my life and I don't see the light any more.

That Black Day

We lived peaceful lives in Darfur and the different tribes generally got along with each other. Arabs from northern Sudan and the African people from southern and western Sudan had lived together for thousands of years. When there were problems, our elders knew how to solve them. The Arabs and Africans in Sudan even intermarried.

I was a young girl and then a young mother, so I wasn't really interested in politics. But I knew that President Omar Hassan Ahmad al-Bashir wasn't good for Sudan. He's the general who grabbed power in 1989.

In 2003 everything began to change in Darfur. No one was safe anymore. The Arab government in Khartoum empowered militias to kill and destroy our people. Sudan is divided between Arab and African tribes. The government supplied the Arab tribes with automatic weapons. Even though in Darfur we are all Muslims, Arab Muslims are killing African Muslims.

The name of these militias is Janjaweed which means 'madman on a horse with a gun.' That's how they call themselves. They're actually trained to kill whomever they want. They come at night, slaughter people, and burn down houses. We had heard about the Janjaweed militias prowling around and killing thousands of people. But we had not experienced their brutality.

Then came that black day.

I stopped typing and my mind wandered to one day when I was visiting Muna's small apartment and the television was on as usual. A double bed for her with purple flowered sheets, a single bed for Mohammed, a large refrigerator, washing machine, television and computer filled most of the space. A world map on the wall decorated their clean and tidy home. Mohammed, sitting in his accustomed spot in front of his computer, was surfing between Facebook and Al Jazeera's sport website.

The television, at a volume too high for my ears, was tuned to Al Jazeera news. Buying a television and ordering a cable or a satellite connection seemed to be one of the first priorities for the Sudanese in Eilat after they received their salaries.

I couldn't understand the Arabic, except for a few words here and there, but suddenly I saw al-Bashir's picture on the screen.

Since we were interested in all news coming from Sudan, I knew that the Chief Prosecutor of the International Criminal Court (ICC) had recently filed charges against al-Bashir for waging genocide through mass murder and rape in Darfur. He asked the judges of the International Criminal Court to issue an arrest warrant for him.

Muna had obviously been following the news also and when she heard the report about al-Bashir she began laughing and cheering. I had never seen her so excited.

On that black day the Janjaweed came to my house. I opened the gate and let them in, still believing that I could reason with them.

They asked, 'Where did your husband get his money?'

How could I answer their accusations? I knew their techniques. In the beginning they kill the educated people and after that the rest of the village. They try to enlist the educated people to help them and if you say anything, they kill you. If you go to the police for help, you find they're against you too.

They went away and I thought we were safe. In my worst nightmares I couldn't have imagined what was coming.

Later I had to go out because Mohammed had a toothache. I took him to a lady in a nearby village who used plants to help with the pain.

While I was gone, the Janjaweed returned. They couldn't actually get near our home because we had a large fenced-in property. In Darfur we have high wooden fences covered with vines and a gate that can only be opened from the inside. This keeps in the animals and keeps out unwanted guests. But they spread gasoline around the perimeter and shot missiles at our house. So my husband and five of my children burned to death, all except for Mohammed.

The Janjaweed ran through our town on horses, shooting and burning, looting and raping, while government planes called

Antonovs bombed us from the sky. When you hear that roar, you know you're in trouble if you don't take cover quickly or try to run away. When people tried to run away, they shot at them. It was awful. I can hardly talk about it.

Those Janjaweed militias killed our whole town and destroyed all the crops. Almost no one came out alive. All my husband's relatives were murdered. Not only that, but they destroyed everything and burned down all our houses. Anyone who wasn't slain ran away from the area.

Nothing remained in our town after the attack on that black day. It was the rainy season when it feels like heaven opens and pours buckets of water down to the earth. Of course normally when it rained I stayed inside with my children. I would enjoy the fresh green smells that the rain brought and look forward to the earth becoming alive.

But that night my son and I ran in the rain and in the darkness. There was no light anywhere. In the rain, our ground becomes muddy and I was tripping and falling a lot. My house dress caught on the bushes and trees. Some of our trees have thorns that are like hooks. When something catches on it, you can't get it loose. I lost all my clothes but had to keep running, moving, flying. Naked! Me, who always wore the beautiful, colorful dresses and scarves common to our tribe. Even after six children, I had always made sure that I looked my best.

Why was I kept alive? I still ask myself. Sometimes I've wished I had died with my husband. But that night I wasn't thinking—I was just fleeing. My son Mohammed was alive and I had to protect him.

Totally exhausted, we finally reached the forest and hid ourselves like wild animals or like cattle that escaped from their owners. Many people from tribes related to the Janjaweed were hunting for us so we were very afraid and remained concealed.

Finally we met a man from our area who took me and Mohammed to his house where his wife gave me some clothes. There I found someone from Zalingei, my husband's hometown.

That man gave us the address of a man called Yahaya and his

wife Fatima and we went to their house. I couldn't even think—I was in shock.

'You're welcome to stay with us,' they said. 'We have clothes for you and Mohammed and money for the way.'

I didn't know Yahaya, but he was from our tribe. That's how it was in those terrible days. People helped each other. When someone ran away, others gave them food, water, clothes and money. They would buy them a train ticket to Khartoum. Our world was falling apart. Our government was against us. But there were individuals who cared for each other.

A week later, we were put under coverings in the bed of a truck on a dark night. We were hiding inside that vehicle as if we were awful criminals, like something the government and the people were trying to throw out. But at least we were getting out of the immediate area, to the city of Nyala.

How has it come to this in just a matter of days? I wondered.

My father and uncle were well respected in our community. My husband was a successful cattle dealer employing other men to work for him. I had lived with him since I was fourteen years old and he always took care of me. Now I was wearing borrowed clothes and hiding in the back of a truck.

Where can I go? I thought. *Who will help me now?*

Tea and Torture in Khartoum

I knew Muna had a horrendous story, but I had no clue of the depth of her suffering—that her husband and five children had been killed by the Janjaweed. I have read many books but had never personally known someone who'd gone through such anguish, except for elderly Holocaust survivors. But for Muna the pain is recent, almost beyond comprehension. Of her six children, only Mohammed survived. No wonder he always looks subdued. What a burden for a young man of 16 to bear, having lost all his siblings and father and to be left alone with his aching, grieving mother.

After transcribing Muna's story on my computer, I wanted to meet her again. I needed to fill in missing details, to ask questions about points I didn't understand. So Moriah made an appointment for us to visit Muna. I asked Joseph to come along to translate.

But how could I ask Muna to tell me more about her dead children? How could I inquire about their personalities, their favorite foods, games and subjects in school? Perhaps some people are able to ask such questions. Maybe you can train yourself to have more of this kind of chutzpah, especially when you know it's for a good purpose, but I don't feel capable.

Joseph, with my prompting, questioned Muna about a few things unclear to me—the sequence of her life in Darfur, some dates and places, the order of her children. But she became annoyed when he seemed to be probing too much. I sensed that she enjoyed speaking and having us listen, but didn't appreciate direct questions.

When I saw Muna a few days later, she told me she didn't want Joseph to come next time, just Moriah and myself. I understood her. She enjoyed hosting us in her home and serving us coke, tea, watermelon and cookies. She also wanted us to bring Nadia, Moriah's friend who studies Arabic and is very sympathetic. Together we managed to understand most of what Muna said in her Arabic/Hebrew using many gestures and repetitions. After several visits I felt I had a grip on the order of the main events of her life.

But the Darfur conflict wasn't getting any simpler in my mind. How can you condense genocide into a neat timeline? As Daoud Hari wrote in *The Translator*, "This isn't a simple genocide, it's a complicated one."

Could any genocide be simple?

*M*ohammed and I stayed hiding in that truck until we reached Nyala, the capital of South Darfur State. Many people don't realize how huge Darfur is and that it's divided into three states— North, West, and South Darfur. Nyala was always a large city and functioned as the center of our region. However, since the

Janjaweed began wreaking their havoc on our villages, thousands of people have fled to Nyala from the surrounding countryside and its population has swelled.

We didn't stay in Nyala. I was looking for protection and safety and couldn't remain in Darfur. So we took the train to Khartoum and arrived after seven days.

In the Nyala train station I met some women, and we decided to travel together for safety and for company. There were fourteen of us from different tribes together with nineteen children including my son, Mohammed, who was then ten years old. Some of the children were those we'd picked up on the way who'd lost their parents.

With nowhere to go when we got off the train, each of us wandered in a different direction. Some of us stayed in the street and others went to the market. Most of us were dressed in rags and were barefoot.

I've escaped the horror of Darfur, I thought, *but now what?* In Sudan our lives revolve around our families and we always take care of each other, but I had no relatives in Khartoum.

There are seven large camps around Khartoum with hundreds of thousands of displaced people. *Should we go to one of those?* I wondered.

Mohammed and I met a man from the Burno tribe. He asked us, 'Where are you from?'

'We've just arrived from Darfur,' I answered.

'Come,' he said. 'Get in my donkey cart and we'll see where you can live. I'll find you some food too.'

He collected blankets and food for us from people in the market. We met him just that one day and then never saw him again.

I went to a camp for internally displaced people in the south of Khartoum. Mayo Mendela, far out in the desert, was as large as a small city. One-story, mud-brick structures stretched in every direction as far as my eye could see.

Is this to be my new home? I thought. *After my lovely, spacious house in Darfur, full of the laughter of happy children?*

But there were no empty houses available and it was September, the rainy season. We had no funds either, because the

Janjaweed stole all the money that the government didn't confiscate from us. I knew though that for Mohammed's sake I had to try my best to provide him with food and shelter to stay alive.

Many of the people living in the camp had escaped from the conflict in southern Sudan and Darfur, but others fled there from Chad, Ethiopia, Uganda and Eritrea—a stew of suffering people. Of course we didn't have enough latrines or water points for everyone, and though diseases spread easily in that environment, we barely had any health services.

Before the first light every morning many of the women left the camp in search of odd jobs. If we were lucky we could find a job cleaning the house of a rich woman or washing her clothes. We might earn one hundred fifty Sudanese dinars a day ($0.50).

One day at the market of Mayo Mandela I found a woman from my tribe. She came to the market daily but lived in Khartoum. 'I can help you get started as a tea seller in the Mayo market,' she suggested. 'I'll give you the tools and then you can begin working.'

I was so thankful to have someone help. I never could have begun on my own. So I joined the other women who worked all day in the market and then I returned to my hut in Mayo Mandela in the evening. I didn't make much money, but at least it was something. I planned to keep working at that job. All I could think about was Mohammed and trying to give him hope for a future.

Many people came to drink my tea. Foreigners and Sudanese aid agency workers came as well as locals. I welcomed everyone and didn't differentiate between nationalities or religions. I didn't realize it at the time, but men from the government security agency also used to stop by my stand. They were watching me, but I didn't suspect them because they weren't wearing uniforms.

One evening, about a month after I began, some Arab men drove up in their car and halted in front of my booth. They jumped out and pointed their guns at me.

'What is your ethnicity?' they asked me harshly. 'From what region do you come?'

I was afraid, although at first I didn't understand who they were or what they wanted. But then I recognized them as security officers from al-Bashir's government.

'Tell us about those Darfur tribes,' they demanded. 'The Tama, Fur, and Zaghawa. Those people who support the Darfur rebel movement.'

Ah, they're here because I'm from Darfur, I realized.

'Why are all the western people drinking tea at your place?' they accused me.

Now I was even more afraid.

'You're operating illegally without a license! Don't you know you're not allowed to sell tea?' They yelled and pushed me into their police car. They seized four other girls also, three from Nuba and one from an Arab tribe.

We began driving, but on the way they stopped and let the three Nubian girls go. After traveling for hours to a place far from our area, they locked us in a house. Later on, they let that Arab girl go and I remained alone.

My thoughts were always for Mohammed. I later learned that he was with Asha during that time, my helpful friend from the market.

My captors moved me around several times, each time grabbing me and forcing me from one car into another. I would have absolutely no idea where they were taking me, because they would blindfold my eyes.

Finally I found myself in a roofless cell so small that I could only stand up, not sit or lie down. In the morning three people came and took me to their office. They sat behind a table and one of them had a cassette recorder.

'We want to know about a leader named Ali Omer,' they demanded, 'and the leaders Oskan and Daoud too.'

They told me these men supported the Darfur rebels.

'Tell us and we'll let you go,' they said.

'Please,' I begged, 'even if you kill me, I have nothing to say. I can't tell you anything about them because I don't know them. I'm just a poor refugee woman selling tea in the market.'

'You're lying!' they screamed. 'We don't believe you!'

I told them that Daoud was from my tribe and during the time

I worked selling tea, he had come to my stand, but I didn't know him personally.

They kept asking me the same questions over and over and I kept giving the same answers. I had nothing else to say.

'Till now we've been nice to you,' they said. 'But if you don't cooperate, soon you'll see our other side.'

They began beating me, kicking me brutally and torturing me all over my body. They forced me to lie down on the ground all night in the rain and in the hot sun every day.

They ripped off all my clothes and tied me up—each leg alone and my arms too.

In her typical demonstrative fashion, Muna raised her arms above her head in a v-shape and spread her legs.

Five men raped me.

I spent four days in the detention cell without food and water. In my pain and delirium I miserably thought, *Why me? What's going to happen to me? No one even knows where I am. I lost my husband, my children and everything. I was finally taking a small step to beginning again and now I'm being abused for no reason.*

After absorbing all those kicks in my stomach, I began to bleed terribly from between my legs. I lost a lot of blood, was very dizzy, and passed out. When the police saw that, they took me outside the detention center and dumped me next to the hospital.

That's where I woke up.

In the morning some young boys on their way to the market found me and carried me into the hospital. But the security forces followed. They ordered me to report to them every Thursday morning and if I didn't cooperate, they would kill me.

I still don't feel well. I hurt everywhere. My head hurts and my arm hurts. I have problems with my nerves. I work cleaning houses as well as in the date packing plant. But it's hard for me to function. I'm always in the health clinic, but the doctors can't find anything wrong with me.

*I*t's hard to identify with statistics. I read that the United Nations estimates at least four hundred thousand people have been killed in Darfur and two and a half million have been displaced as of October 2006[1]. Many call the attack in Darfur genocide, including the United States government, the International Criminal Court and the U.S. Holocaust Museum[2]. Over one hundred eighty faith-based humanitarian and human rights organizations have formed an alliance called Save Darfur[3]. The conflict in Sudan has been called the 'world's worst humanitarian crisis' by the outgoing United Nations Resident and Humanitarian Coordinator for Sudan, Mukesh Kapila[4].

Our inability to identity with numbers is why Yad Vashem, Israel's Holocaust Museum, launched a campaign called "Unto Every Person There is a Name." The aim is to collect the names of every man, woman and child killed during the Holocaust because the Nazis took away the names of their victims and replaced them with numbers. This project commemorates each person and returns their identities. On Holocaust Remembrance Day in Israel, their names are read aloud.

Hearing Muna tell her story—giving her a platform—put a personal face for me on the Darfur tragedy. Muna isn't a statistic.

I came to understand it wasn't a coincidence that the hostilities in Darfur accelerated at the time that the peace talks began seriously in the south. The Darfur rebels began their fight because Darfur had been left out of the wealth and power sharing agreements between the government and the southern Sudanese rebels.

The future for the millions of south Sudanese as well as Darfurian refugees remains uncertain, and if we look at Sudan's record since independence in 1956 we won't find much reason for optimism. Yet for Muna and Mohammed's sake I keep hoping and praying for peace and security in their blood-stained homeland.

---

1. http://www.darfurscores.org/darfur
2. http://news.bbc.co.uk/2/hi/africa/3918765.stm
3. www.savedarfur.org
4. http://news.bbc.co.uk/2/hi/africa/3549325.stm

Living in Israel we're used to looking for miracles in the midst of depressing circumstances. We understand there are no simple political solutions.

Next Destination – Saudi Arabia or Israel

When I was released from the hospital, I went home, desperate to find Mohammed. My friends asked where I'd been. They were afraid I'd been run over and killed. I told them everything that had happened to me since the security men abducted me from my tea stand.

Although I was broken in spirit and in body, I knew I couldn't stay in Khartoum any longer. The police were looking for me. So Asha secretively took Mohammed and me to an open field north of Khartoum where others from my tribe were camping. Thankfully, I met a man who could secure passports for Mohammed and me. In Sudan you can do that—pay a bribe and get a passport. I gave him photos of us and in two weeks we had passports and tickets to leave Sudan. My age on the passport wasn't correct; I was born in 1969 but the passport said 1963.

One night Mohammed and I boarded the train to Wadi Halfa on the Sudanese and Egyptian border. We traveled in the railroad car for animals. From Wadi Halfa we took a steamer across Lake Nasser, hiding inside a storage room for two days until we reached Egypt in March 2004. I thanked God that I was out of Sudan and safely across the border.

So we finally arrived in Cairo, longing to begin a new life. After losing my children and husband and suffering torture, I was looking for safety and protection. Unfortunately, I quickly discovered that the Egyptian people don't want Sudanese refugees in their land, and life wasn't any better than in Sudan. I found a job cleaning houses, but as I walked on the street I was beaten and insulted for no reason other than for being black.

When riding on a bus one day, men started grabbing my breasts.

In Muna's typical way, she demonstrated on herself, and began acting out both the man's and her role.

They took off their shoes and beat me. In the Arab culture to hit someone with your shoe is awful. You're not even supposed to show people the bottom of your sole because it's dirty.

Life in Egypt was unbearable. I couldn't afford to buy food for Mohammed and myself and to pay rent for a room in a slum. I suffered from many physical problems. Thankfully I heard about a Christian hospital in Cairo, the only one willing to examine me. People from all over—Iraq, Palestine, Oman and Somalia—received treatment for free. I had an operation on my stomach to correct the result of the beatings in the detention center, and the kind doctors gave me medicine.

I was afraid to stay alone with my son because of the stories I heard about Egyptians abducting women and children. So I contacted a man who said he had known my husband.

'I'm willing to marry you,' he told me. 'You and Mohammed will move into my house and I'll care for you.'

I agreed and he registered me at the UNHCR as part of his family. When I had applied earlier for Mohammed and me, they wouldn't accept us.

In 2005 this man escaped to the U.S. without even telling me he was going to leave. At first he would call me from America, but when I kept telling him that I was sick with stomach pains because of the beatings in Khartoum, he stopped contacting me. So I was alone again with Mohammed. And because I had no money, our landlord threw me out onto the street.

We Sudanese refugees were asking the United Nations to give us asylum in other countries, like the United States or Australia, but they didn't seem to be trying to help. So we set up a protest camp in front of the UN headquarters.

In late December 2005 after several hundred of us had been

there for three months already, peacefully demonstrating and demanding our rights, I felt the tension rising. I could feel something was about to happen.

'Go away somewhere!' I warned Mohammed. We had some friends in an apartment close by. I wanted Mohammed to be safe, but I felt I should stay behind with my friends, not realizing yet how violently we would be attacked.

Three thousand armed Egyptian police surrounded us and began beating and shooting. They sprayed us with water hoses. I think there was poison in that water because afterwards I became very sick. I was beaten on my stomach. I saw babies trampled by horses.

Soldiers came and ordered us to get in their car. We refused because we knew they were taking us away to kill us. 'Just shoot us here, in front of the United Nations,' we dared them. 'Then the entire world will see.'

I ran away to the apartment where Mohammed was. But dozens of women and children were killed that day.

Our situation as refugees became worse. I decided to go to the Saudi Arabian Embassy because I heard they helped needy people, especially widows and orphans. My mother was born in Saudi Arabia. I took a bus because the embassy was far away and I could barely walk with all my pain. But I was determined and was sure that I would be helped.

'What are you doing here?' the embassy's secretary asked me harshly. 'Where are you from?'

'I'm from Darfur, in western Sudan,' I answered. 'My late husband was from the same region.'

When they heard that, they started screaming at me. Then one of those clerks called me a prostitute and compared me to a shoe. I began to cry. Those Saudis are so proud!

What is my crime except for being a poor and needy widow? I thought.

My mother was much honored; my father had a lot of money and gold; in Sudan I had a good name, but in Egypt they compared me to a shoe! I had no value at all to them.

'Get out of here!' they yelled. 'You're an infidel. You call yourself a Muslim, but what kind of religion do you follow? Your form of Islam is worse than being an unbeliever.'

Though they didn't hit my physically, I felt as though I was being slapped. I hurt in my heart.

They called the Egyptian police who took me to the police station, but thank God I met a kind officer there. I told him about my desperate situation. I had no food for my son and myself, and I showed him the medical report about my stomach operation. He released me.

But where could I go?

Although I am a Muslim, I decided to go to the Christian Zamelek church. Even in the Mandela Mayo camp outside of Khartoum there were sixty nine Christian organizations but only three Islamic associations. Yet many of the people being served were Muslims. I discovered that Christians don't discriminate according to religion.

I had no home, no work, and no money. All I had was Mohammed, bread and tea. That's it—no other food, no milk. So I went to the only place I knew where they would take care of me—the Christian church in Zamelek. I met some kind Sudanese women who arranged for me to receive olive oil, sugar, clothes and 500 Egyptian pounds (about $100).

Though emotionally and physically exhausted, I was completely overwhelmed by their kindness. I began crying. A wonderful woman from Australia who worked at the church came to talk to me. I really loved that woman—even though she was white, she treated me well. I'll never forget how she made me feel so special. I was weeping and she put her arms around me.

'Sorry, sorry,' we mumbled to each other in one of the few words we both understood. I couldn't speak English and she couldn't speak Arabic.

I cried and cried.

'Where are you from?' she asked through an interpreter.

'I'm from Sudan.'

'A Muslim from Darfur?'

'Yes. In Sudan they want to kill me.'

Muna frowned, put her fingers together and swiped them across her neck, as if slitting her throat.

'*I* have been in Egypt for a year and a half,' I told her. 'People beat me here on the street. In the Saudi embassy they called me a prostitute. This church is the only place that has helped me.'

'You must leave Egypt,' she and other people at the church told me.

'But I have no money.'

'We'll help you go to Israel,' they proposed. 'That's the only option where you'll be safe.' I received an envelope from the church with $300 for the journey.

I went home that night and was finally able to sleep well. I had peace in my heart. I was going to Israel!

Everyone is Nice

Muna always received us so warmly and seemed to genuinely enjoy our visits. The next time I visited, still feeling the need for more details of her story, I took with me Salaam, an Arab Christian friend from the Galilee area now living in Eilat, who speaks Hebrew as well as Arabic.

Salaam, a warm, friendly woman, knew Muna and quickly put her at ease. I brought along a printed copy of my manuscript for reference and through Salaam asked Muna to clarify certain points. The two women launched into a lively discussion and I faded into the background.

As I sat there, I observed how Muna had enlarged her small home by annexing the apartment next door and putting a door between them. Now she and Mohammed each had their own room.

I divided my attention between attempting to pick up the occasional Arabic word that I recognized, following Muna's body language, and watching the over-dramatic Arab soap opera on the television.

Every ten minutes or so, Salaam seemed to remember my presence and halted their dialogue to interpret for me. I wrote down Muna's words in my version of shorthand.

When the story reached the time of her torture in Khartoum, Muna was crying and Salaam was crying with her.

Then she recovered enough to tell the rest of her story.

I sold our few clothes, took my son and left for Israel in August 2006. We drove to El Arish in northern Sinai and some Bedouins drove us through the desert to the Israeli border. They wrapped Mohammed and me in sheets in the back of their truck. Of course I was afraid, but I was so happy to be leaving Egypt. I had nothing with me except my passport and our UN document.

After driving for hours, we finally stepped out of the Bedouin's truck in the dark and began walking over the rocky ground and climbing up and down mountains in the direction they pointed out to us. My stomach was swollen and painful. I don't know how I had the strength.

Suddenly I could see the fence in front of us. 'Come, Mohammed!' I yelled as we got closer and began running.

'Mama!' he screamed and grabbed my scarf.

The Egyptian soldiers began shouting and throwing stones at us. With all my remaining power I lifted the barbed wire fence for Mohammed to pass under. My documents fell and when I turned around to retrieve them, a stone thrown by one of the soldiers smashed into my head. Blood ran down my face.

'Run! Run, Mohammed!' I cried again and then we were across.

The Egyptians couldn't run after us because of the Israeli soldiers on the other side. It was 3:00 A.M. I was terribly weak because of the running and from my operation. My eye and mouth were swollen from that rock the Egyptian threw. My skin was covered with scratches from the barbed wire and my clothes were torn in shreds. I collapsed and fell to the ground.

Two Israeli police came. They carried me in their arms.

'Who are you?' they gently asked, calling me 'mother.' The police were nice. Everyone was nice. I hadn't eaten for two days and they gave me cookies, cola and juice.

They behaved so kindly. They took Mohammed and me to a hospital. A doctor examined my swollen stomach and treated us.

After the doctor pronounced me well enough to leave, the police took us to an army camp. Mohammed and I were put together in one room with a television. We stayed there for two weeks until they took us to Tel Aviv where we stayed in a women's shelter for twenty days. Then they put Mohammed, me and four other Sudanese on a bus for the five hour trip through the desert to Kibbutz Eilot.

I don't want to go to any place else because I like the people on the kibbutz. They speak kindly to me and always greet me. I'm happy in Israel.

The next time I met Muna she looked radiant. She had straightened her hair and for the first time I saw her without a scarf.

It was Mohammed's seventeenth birthday party as well as the celebration of two years since he and his mother, Muna, had arrived in Israel. Muna invited Sudanese friends from the kibbutz, other Darfurian friends, and a number of Israelis for an outdoor feast. Tables were laid with all sorts of cakes, cookies and soft drinks. Several Sudanese musicians set up a keyboard and drums and to my surprise, Muna was singing!

Epilog

I'm able to work in Israel and everyone treats Mohammed and me with respect. Not like in Egypt. I have made good friends and others have become like family to me. Mohammed goes to an

Israeli high school and speaks Hebrew well.

I'm happy in Israel because I don't hear the sound of guns. I'm not afraid here. But every day I remember my husband and five children who were killed by the Janjaweed in Darfur … and the abuse I suffered in Khartoum and in Cairo. I'm always worried and have trouble sleeping. I go often to the doctor and have many pains. I sometimes have to crawl to the bathroom in the middle of the night.

I am looking for protection as a refugee because I have nothing to go back to in Sudan. I want to stay in a good place without the noise of guns like in Darfur. I am worried about my future because I don't want to hear shooting all of my life.

When I work I send money to my mother. She's eighty two years old and lives in Sudan near the Ethiopian border. She takes care of the eight children of my brother. My brother has lost an arm, so he can't work.

I worry about my mother and those children. I dream of resettling in America and bringing my nieces and nephew with me. I would adopt them, and my mother wouldn't be so burdened.

But Israel is good. It's good here for the Sudanese. Thanks to all the Israeli leaders and the government, because they are good people. God be with you.

Muna's story is different than that of the south Sudanese refugees. From the beginning, the Darfurians have received more public sympathy due to the fact that their conflict is regarded as genocide by many countries and organizations.

In July 2007 Israel granted citizenship to five hundred refugees from Darfur. As Interior Minister Meir Sheetrit said, "Because of the history of the Jewish people themselves, Israel cannot ignore the (Darfur) refugees' fate." (Haaretz.com, June 12, 2007)

Muna and Mohammed are two beneficiaries of this edict. Their status in Israel is secure and not left up to the whims of the changing Israeli governments.

They still live on the kibbutz but have enlarged their home

by annexing the next-door apartment and enclosing their porch. Mohammed attends the local high school where he is the only Sudanese in his class.

Israeli high schools have a tradition of sending the eleventh or twelfth grade students on trips to Poland in order to understand the Holocaust in a more personal way. Mohammed was featured in Israeli newspapers when he was able to receive a laissez-passer to join his classmates. The article, which appeared on www.ynetnews.com dated July 3, 2010 under the headline, "Darfur teen to visit Auschwitz" stated:

Muhammad, who escaped Sudan genocide and found shelter in Israel, [is] to travel to Nazi concentration camp with his classmates.

'Studying about your Holocaust helps me connect to my own holocaust,' he tells his friends.

Kibbutz Eilot's eleventh graders are scheduled to visit Auschwitz this month. They will stand at the former Nazi concentration camp and try to imagine the last moments of the Jewish victims, who saw their loved ones being murdered before their eyes. Unfortunately, one of the journey's participants will not have to use his imagination.

Muhammad and his mother escaped from Darfur, a western Sudan region which has become one of the world's most shocking locations of a humanitarian disaster. Some seven hundred thousand people have been slaughtered there since 2003 by militia groups and rebels, and millions have escaped and turned into refugees.

I was so proud of Mohammed and Muna when I happened across the article, and I immediately called Muna in case she hadn't heard about it yet. I imagined what an asset it must have been to the high school group to have Mohammed with them.

Mohammed is in his senior year and is studying for the matriculation exams with the rest of his class. When I asked him about his plans for next year he told me, "I'll be doing a year of national service."

Most Israeli youth are inducted into the Israeli Defense Forces upon completion of high school. Some, either because of health issues or because they want to give something back to the community before serving in the army, elect to do "national service."

"What will you be doing?" I asked.

"I'll be a teacher for young children in Rishon LeTzion (a city near Tel Aviv)." He made a troubled face. "It's hard to be a teacher."

"Wow, that's wonderful!" I said. "A teacher is one of the most important jobs there is. You're able to guide children and influence them. I'm sure you'll do fine."

Again I was proud of Mohammed and wondered if Muna understood what an exceptional son she had.

On September 9, 2009 Muna married Ahmed, another refugee from Darfur, in a moving ceremony in Kibbutz Eilot. Muna looked stunning in a dazzling pink wedding dress and an elaborate hairdo with hundreds of fine braids. Meeting Ahmed for the first time in his dark suit, I had the impression of a kind and serious man.

Viewing the two of them sitting side by side on the red velvet covered podium brought tears to my eyes as I reflected on how far Muna had come to reach this point in her life. And I prayed that God would now grant her rest and peace to somehow make up for all her suffering.

When I visited her recently, she spoke in her own style of half-Hebrew, half-Arabic. "I'm working in another job now." She said. She was lying in bed and invited me to sit next to her. "I have high blood pressure and a terrible headache, but the pills I take usually help."

Muna continued, "I talk often to my mother and sister in Sudan." Muna wiped a tear from her eye. "And I send them money from my salary every month."

When I saw her husband, Ahmed, typing a document on his laptop for the organization of Darfur refugees, I discovered that he speaks both English and Hebrew.

"What do you think about the referendum in south Sudan?"

I asked him. "It should eventually help you in Darfur as well, right?"

Ahmed gave a large smile. "Sure. We're happy for it. We're thankful it's been going well so far. Things could have gone much worse."

"Al Bashir said that he'll respect the results of the referendum and allow south Sudan to separate," I noted.

"I don't believe him," Muna said. She touched her mouth and then her heart. "He talks with his mouth, but what about his heart?"

"We'll just hope he does what he says," I said.

"At least he said it," added Ahmed.

"Inshallah!" I said.

"Inshallah!" they both repeated.

6. Conclusion

John and a Sudanese man visiting Jerusalem

I Would Not Have Believed Them

One day John shook his head and looked at me, saying, "If someone had told me a few years ago that we'd be involved with Sudanese people, I would not have believed them."

I had to agree.

Throughout the experience of working with them and getting to know them, our Sudanese friends have taught me so much about maintaining a positive attitude and not worrying about the future. I've also discovered many traits in myself, both positive and negative, of which I wasn't aware.

We encountered challenges. For instance, when faced with people who truly have nothing—no material possessions and no home to return to—how much are we willing to give of our time and possessions? For those Sudanese who call themselves Christians but certainly don't act like followers of the Messiah, how can we help hold them accountable, especially when we don't understand their culture and language? Even John and I, and our children who are deeply involved in the work with the refugees, do not agree on all the answers to these questions.

After several months of intense involvement with the refugees we noticed that the teenagers and children were the most open, the most needy, and had the most free time.

Groups of ten or more boys began coming to our house every afternoon. John loved feeding them—pita and humus, leftovers, or just juice and cookies. Gradually they all acquired bicycles, their new status symbol, and zoomed around town like teenagers with their first cars.

Our house was their clubhouse and our yard their parking lot and repair shop. Most of the time we didn't mind the chaos and noise. If the boys weren't with us, where else would they go? Hang out on the street? Their homes were tiny and their parents at work.

Our neighbors, however, saw things differently.

"Listen. I haven't mentioned this to you till now, but it's really too much. That you want to help all the poor Africans in town, that's your business. But not at our expense. My baby can't fall asleep with all the racket coming from your house. Those bikes are close to her room."

"Abba, she's right," our oldest daughter, Racheli, said. "We can't live like this. We need to set boundaries. These boys aren't worse behaved than most Israeli teenagers, but no one would like this racket next to their house."

The following day when the boys showed up, John shared with them the disappointing news: they'd have to find someplace else to park their bikes. Quiet returned to our neighborhood and we were learning lessons about how to balance helping the refugees with consideration for our neighbors and maintaining our own personal space.

Another question arose: Is it helpful to give indiscriminately or, even when they have so much less than we have, should we temper our giving in order not to create a dependency?

The Sudanese attitude toward possessions is different from ours. In the beginning we had a hard time contacting individuals because they didn't have phones yet. When we organized events, they were delighted with the photos we took. But we noticed that after they received salaries and bought cell phones, many were the expensive models with cameras. Soon they were taking more pictures than we were.

One Sudanese explained that when they were living in Sudan they didn't use money. Their wealth was measured in cows and they had mostly a barter economy. So when they receive a paycheck, they see no reason to save. Money is meaningless for them and they may as well spend it. I wondered about all the years they lived in Egypt. Did that not teach them to spend money wisely? Did that cause more problems for them in Egypt too?

"Abba, you shouldn't keep bringing clothes to the Sudanese," our youngest daughter, Moriah, cautioned us. "They have enough. Most of them dress nicer than we do."

"There are always people who take the clothes," John answered. Because it's deeply rooted in John's nature to give, it's hard for him to see things differently.

"And those food coupons you give them," added Moriah, "I've seen them in the supermarket buying beer. Did you know they can also use them in the upscale clothing stores?"

After the initial period when the refugees came to us for all their needs—food, medicine, dentist, clothing—and we gave almost indiscriminately, we discovered the system of food coupons. Bought in the supermarket, they can be spent like money. The problem is that they are good not only for food, but for liquor which is also sold in the grocery stores. And in the small print on the back of the coupons is a long list of other shops where they can be redeemed.

How can we help the Sudanese to assimilate into our modern society while not forgetting their culture and roots? Not knowing whether they'll remain in Israel makes this dilemma more difficult. We don't have the answers and even when we think we know what we're doing, we may change our minds the next week.

Several trends are unequivocal—the number of refugees crossing the border is skyrocketing, and they are falling out of favor in the eyes of the average Israeli.

As of December 2010, there are estimates of over thirty thousand African migrants residing in Israel: sixty percent from Eritrea, another repressive East African nation, thirty percent from Sudan, and the rest from other African countries. We've heard that there are still a thousand Africans crossing the border every month.

One sign of the change in Israeli attitude is the vocabulary used. Whereas they were at first called "refugees," now the media refers to them as "infiltrators" or "migrants" with the implication that they are coming for economic reasons, not to seek asylum.

While even in the beginning most Israelis weren't thrilled to have African refugees entering our country illegally, due to our history many felt a kinship for those fleeing religious repression. Human rights groups were able to arouse sympathy and many people were moved to lend a hand.

As the trickle has grown to a tsunami with no end in sight, and the Africans are becoming an inescapable presence particularly in the poor neighborhoods of Eilat and Tel Aviv, Israel has joined other Western countries in being forced to deal with this complicated situation. This phenomenon challenges many developed nations and governments, including the United States, Europe, and Australia.

Till recently Israel had been spared this scenario and was able to get by with a policy of "no policy." It's easier to pretend the refugee problem doesn't exist than to take concrete action. Even those who believe we should help these refugees recognize that Israel cannot simply open the borders and allow any African searching for a better life to come here. Israel, a nation of seven million people, would be swamped by millions of desperate Africans.

Yet neither can we ignore the several thousands who have made the dangerous journey through the desert to reach Israel. They have no place to return. Sudan considers Israel their enemy, so to send refugees back to their homeland is a death sentence.

Much ignorance exists in Israel considering the loyalties of the Sudanese refugees.

"Aren't they all Muslims who support Hamas and Hizbullah?" I've been asked.

In fact, whether they are Christians from south Sudan or Muslims from Darfur, they have a fierce dislike for the Arab Muslims due to all the persecution and suffering they've experienced. The Christians identify with the children of Israel leaving Egypt for the Promised Land, but even the Sudanese Muslims are aware that no Muslim country offered them assistance. Most would be happy to stay in Israel at least until there is peace in south Sudan and Darfur, and then they hope to return home.

I am upset that Israel's government differentiates between the Darfur refugees and those from south Sudan. Because Darfur was in the news when the refugees arrived, and the word "genocide" was being used, Israelis couldn't ignore these desperate people. The refugees from the south who had been suffering for years were easier to disregard.

The Israeli government quickly gave temporary residency status to the Darfur refugees whereas the south Sudanese are in limbo and remain dependent on the United Nations.

Our south Sudanese friends told us they are disappointed because Darfurians aided the government troops in their campaign against south Sudan.

"So why does the Israeli government give preference to the Darfur refugees?" they ask. And I have no answer.

Belatedly, in the fall of 2010 Prime Minister Netanyahu's government developed a threefold strategy to address this refugee "catastrophe" as they call it. First of all, a fence is being built along the Egyptian border to stop more Africans from entering Israel. Secondly, they plan to build a large detention facility near the border, capable of holding ten thousand people. And third would be strict enforcement against Israeli employers who hire the refugees/migrants.

Needless to say, the hostility between the two Israeli groups (pro- and anti-refugee) is only likely to grow.

The other big question mark in the equation is the referendum in Sudan. Four million registered south Sudanese voters on January 9, 2011 chose between continued unity with the north or separation and independence. Assuming the voting goes relatively smoothly and the north accepts the outcome—expected to be secession—the challenges facing the new country will be enormous.

Southern Sudan, a Texas-sized territory of an estimated 8.7 million people, is among the world's poorest, least healthy, and least educated countries (*Yahoo News*, January 6, 2011). Life expectancy in south Sudan is forty-two years old, and one in ten children die before their first birthday. The literacy rate is the second lowest in the world, after Afghanistan, with an average of five percent finishing elementary school. Boreholes and unprotected wells are their main drinking sources and eighty percent of the population has no toilet facilities (*BBC News*, January 4, 2011).

The UN says that a typical fifteen-year-old girl has a higher chance of dying in childbirth than finishing school. Aid groups say southerners streaming home from the north are creating dire shortages of basic services (*Yahoo News*).

Despite these depressing statistics, several hundred of the south Sudanese living in Israel chose to return to their homeland in the latter part of 2010. An international aid organization cooperating with the UN is enabling those who decide to go back to Sudan.

If asked, most Sudanese say they hope to go home, but the unfolding climate for the refugees in Israel as well as the political situation in south Sudan will influence their timing.

I wish these stories had a tidy conclusion, such as: The Israeli government decided to grant residency to all the Sudanese refugees and they are successfully integrating into Israeli society. Or: Peace has been established in south Sudan and Darfur and the refugees are all happily and safely on their way home.

Unfortunately neither of these scenarios appears realistic at this time. The situation of the Sudanese refugees in Israel remains in limbo. The Darfurians, due to the genocide in their homeland, have been granted temporary residency, but the south Sudanese are still caught up in the process of renewing their UN refugee documents every couple of months.

This isn't the first time that they've lived with uncertainty. As refugees, they have spent more of their lives in a state of insecurity than in being able to plan their future. In general, they are basically resilient and optimistic people, though. They've had to be. When your world comes crashing down and you lose everything and everyone dear to you, you learn to live for today and hope for a better tomorrow.

A herd of cattle belonging to the Dinka tribe, on a road in south Sudan
(iStockPhoto)

Glossary

abuna. Literally 'our father'; also a title used among Arabic-speaking Christians to refer to a priest.

animist. One who worships animals and other natural objects and phenomena which they believe represent "spirits."

antonov. A Russian-built aircraft often used for bombing civilian targets in Sudan.

baba. "Father" in Arabic.

bedouin. A desert-dwelling Arab ethnic group.

bush. Rural, undeveloped land and forest.

chutzpah. Slang from Yiddish: audacity, nerve.

chukran. "Thank you" in Arabic

djellabah (or jalabiya). A loose-fitting robe worn by Arab men.

Druze. A monotheistic religious group in Israel with an Arabic culture and language.

ful. Fava beans or broad beans, a common staple in the Egyptian diet.

IDF. Israeli Defense Forces.

Inshallah. "God willing" in Arabic.

IOM. International Office for Migration, an intergovernmental organization

jalabiya (or djellabah). A loose fitting robe worn by Arab men.

Janjaweed. Armed group of gunmen in Darfur.

junta. Committee, such as a board of directors.

kibbutz (kibbutzim). A collective community in Israel.

maize. A type of corn, the most widely grown crop in Africa.

mandazi. East African fried breads similar to doughnuts.

m'luchiya. Leaves of mallow (a wild plant with green, edible leaves).

moshav (moshavim). An Israeli cooperative agricultural community.

muezzin. A chosen person at the mosque who leads the call to Friday service and the five daily prayers from one of the mosque's minarets.

mujahideen. Islamic terrorists.

NGO. Non-Governmental Organization.

Nilotic. Ethnic groups from the Nile River basin.

sharia. A body of Islamic religious law based on the Koran.

SPLA. Sudanese People's Liberation Army, the predominantly Christian rebel movement based in southern Sudan.

todah. Thank you (Hebrew).

ugali. A porridge-like side dish made with cooked cornmeal.

ulpan. A school for the intensive study of Hebrew.

UNHCR. The United Nations High Commissioner for Refugees, a UN agency mandated to protect and support refugees.

shuk. An outdoor marketplace.

Resources for Further Reading

Ajak, Benjamin, and Benson Deng, Alephonsion Deng, Judy Bernstein. *They Poured Fire on us From the Sky: The Story of Three Lost Boys from Sudan*. PublicAffairs, 2006.

Bixler, Mark. *The Lost Boys of Sudan: An American Story of the Refugee Experience*. University of Georgia Press, 2006.

Dau, John Bul with Michael S. Sweeney. *God Grew Tired of Us: A Memoir*. National Geographic, 2007.

Eggers, Dave. *What is the What: The Autobiography of Valentino Achak Deng*. McSweeney's, 2006.

Hari, Daoud. *The Translator: A Tribesman's Memoir of Darfur*. Random House, 2008.

Hecht, Joan. *The Journey of the Lost Boys: A Story of Courage, Faith and the Sheer Determination to Survive by a Group of Young Boys Called "The Lost Boys of Sudan"*. Allswell Press, 2005.

Nhial, Abraham and DiAnn Mills. *Lost Boy No More: A True Story of Survival and Salvation*. B&H Books, 2004.

Marlowe, Jen with Aisha Bain and Adam Shapiro. *Darfur Diaries: Stories of Survival*. Nation Books, 2006.

Assaf (Aid Organization for Refugees and Asylum Seekers in Israel): http://www.assaf.org.il/en/

Hotline for Migrant Workers: http://www.hotline.org.il/english/index.htm

Kav LaOved (Worker's Hotline) http://www.kavlaoved.org.il/default_eng.asp

Physicians for Human Rights - Israel: http://www.phr.org.il/default.asp?PageID=4

Acknowledgments

I didn't plan on writing a book about the Sudanese. I thought I would write about the Shelter Hostel with a chapter on the Sudanese—the most recent people group to pass through our hostel. While reading books about Sudan and the Lost Boys in order to understand the background of our new friends, I became convinced that the story of the Sudanese in Eilat deserved its own book and that God could use me to write it. He inspired me, gave me the idea for the book's structure, led me to the right people, and helped me with every step.

I want to thank the Sudanese community for including us in their lives. Especially I thank Gabriel, Muna and Andrew, Rose, Muna from Darfur, and Yien for uncovering their often painful pasts to me. They patiently explained, gave of their time, answered my questions, and shared their tears.

My family is an inseparable part of my identity and of this book. John had the vision and heart to get involved with the refugees. He encouraged me to write their stories and our story. He freed time for me and understood things I overlooked. Our children, Josh, Racheli, Moriah and Yonatan, and their spouses, Sarah and Tom, were always available to listen and cheer me on.

Salaam was more than a translator. She not only interpreted Rose's and Muna's stories from Arabic to Hebrew so I could write them in English, but she also instinctively knew what questions to ask and how to ask them.

My writers' group—Faith, Ruth, Zela and Betsy—made the isolated occupation of a writer feel a little less lonely. Encouraging words from veteran writers, Eric, Kay, and Jen, as well as my sister Jane, lifted my spirits.

Thanks to my parents, Harry and Velma Galblum, for encouraging and believing in me and always asking about this book. They are an inspiration of tolerance and commitment to all their family and friends.

I thank Catherine Lawton, my publisher, for taking on this book, and Christina Slike, my editor, for the hours of work you contributed to make it a much better product.

When we began to get involved with the Sudanese, I never imagined we would end up with two little Sudanese grandsons, Daniel and Sunday, ages six and eight. Lively, cute, inquisitive, friendly, and affectionate, they became the foster children of Moriah and Tom. I thank these children for teaching me lessons about day-by-day living and trust.

About the Author

Judith Galblum Pex was born in Washington, D.C., but has lived with her husband, John, in Eilat, Israel, since 1976. Twenty-six years ago John and Judith began the Shelter Hostel, a guest house for travelers from all over the world and a drop-in center for anyone searching for physical, emotional, or spiritual support. John, from Holland, is the pastor of the Eilat Congregation, a multi-cultural, non-denominational fellowship.

Judith and John are the parents of four grown children, two of whom are married. All the children live in Israel. In her free time Judith likes to read, hike and camp in the mountains around Eilat, and to snorkel in the Red Sea.

Judith is also the author of *Walk the Land: A Journey on Foot through Israel* (Cladach).

All of the author's proceeds from the sales of *A People Tall and Smooth* will go to projects for the Sudanese refugees.

Learn more and get updates at www.judithpex.com.